T0260237

Getting Started with Flex™ 3

Getting Started with Flex™ 3

Jack Herrington and Emily Kim

O'REILLY®

Beijing · Cambridge · Farnham · Köln · Sebastopol · Taipei · Tokyo

Getting Started with Flex˜ 3
by Jack Herrington and Emily Kim

Published by O'Reilly Media, Inc., 1005 Gravenstein Highway North, Sebastopol, CA 95472.

O'Reilly books may be purchased for educational, business, or sales promotional use. Online editions are also available for most titles (*http://safari.oreilly.com*). For more information, contact our corporate/institutional sales department: (800) 998-9938 or *corporate@oreilly.com*.

Editor: Steve Weiss
Copy Editor: Audrey Doyle
Proofreader: Carol Marti
Indexer: Joe Wizda
Cover Designer: Karen Montgomery
Illustrators: Robert Romano and Jessamyn Read

Printing History:

    June 2008:   First Edition

ISBN: 978-0-596-52064-9

[T]   [11/08]

1225468376

Adobe Developer Library, a copublishing partnership between O'Reilly Media Inc., and Adobe Systems, Inc., is the authoritative resource for developers using Adobe technologies. These comprehensive resources offer learning solutions to help developers create cutting-edge interactive web applications that can reach virtually anyone on any platform.

With top-quality books and innovative online resources covering the latest tools for rich-Internet application development, the *Adobe Developer Library* delivers expert training straight from the source. Topics include ActionScript, Adobe Flex®, Adobe Flash®, and Adobe Acrobat®.

Get the latest news about books, online resources, and more at *http://adobedeveloperlibrary.com*.

Contents

Preface

How many times have you gotten an idea for a killer application in your mind, only to have the implementation fail when the framework you use bogs you down in the detail work? I know I certainly have experienced that. Fortunately, Flex came to my rescue and made the process of implementing my ideas fun again. I can think up amazing interfaces and pull them together quickly in Flex. While I concentrate on the design, Flex handles all the details of making it happen.

This book will inspire you to try Flex and to see just how much fun it can be to bring your ideas to life. Let Flex make your interface design and coding enjoyable again!

Who Should Read This Book

This book is primarily intended for people who are new to Flex or who have tried previous versions of Flex and are interested in what's new in Flex 3. I've designed the book to be a *quick tour* of the Flex world without delving too deeply into any one topic. To provide in-depth coverage of every topic I present in the book would require five times the page count, which could present a health hazard to you, dear reader.

To make up for the lack of depth in every area, in Chapter 10 I provide a collection of resources from which you can glean additional information regarding Flex. And as always, there is

Google, which is your best friend when it comes to learning about the nooks and crannies of the Flex API.

How This Book Is Organized

Here is a summary of the chapters in the book and what you can expect from each:

Chapter 1
> In this chapter, I'll guide you through installing Flex Builder 3 and putting together a fun image manipulator application.

Chapter 2
> This chapter presents several real-world examples of sites that make amazing use of Flex.

Chapter 3
> This chapter provides a step-by-step walkthrough of how to build a Flex application.

Chapter 4
> This chapter describes Flex layout mechanisms and controls. Filters and effects are also covered.

Chapter 5
> This chapter covers the different forms of network communications supported by Flex applications, and includes examples for a few of them.

Chapter 6
> This chapter presents additional example applications, including a calculator, an image viewer, a drag-and-drop application, and more.

Chapter 7
> This chapter provides a preview of several advanced controls that are available for use as stock libraries. Some choice examples include 3D graphing, as well as a flow list that is similar to Cover Flow in iTunes.

Chapter 8

> This chapter discusses how to build small Flex movies for use on other people's web pages. A full working chat widget is provided as an example.

Chapter 9

> This chapter covers how to use Adobe's AIR runtime to put Flex applications on the desktop.

Chapter 10

> This chapter presents numerous resources for Flex developers, including blogs, forums, podcasts, books, and more.

Conventions Used in This Book

The following typographical conventions are used in this book:

Italic

> Indicates new terms, URLs, email addresses, filenames, file extensions, pathnames, directories, and Unix utilities

`Constant width`

> Indicates commands, options, switches, variables, attributes, keys, functions, types, classes, namespaces, methods, modules, properties, parameters, values, objects, events, event handlers, XML tags, HTML tags, macros, the contents of files, and the output from commands

`Constant width bold`

> Shows commands or other text that should be typed literally by the user

Constant width italic

> Shows text that should be replaced with user-supplied values

How to Contact Us

Please address comments and nontechnical questions concerning this book to the publisher:

O'Reilly Media, Inc.
1005 Gravenstein Highway North
Sebastopol, CA 95472
800-998-9938 (in the United States or Canada)
707-829-0515 (international or local)
707-829-0104 (fax)

We have a web page for this book, where we list errata, examples, and any additional information. You can access this page at:

http://www.oreilly.com/catalog/9780596520649

For more information about our books, conferences, Resource Centers, and the O'Reilly Network, see our website at:

http://www.oreilly.com

About the Author

Jack Herrington is an engineer, author, and presenter who lives and works in the San Francisco Bay area with his wife, daughter, and two dogs. He is the author of three additional books, *Code Generation In Action*, *Podcasting Hacks*, and *PHP Hacks*, as well as numerous articles. You can check out his technical blog at *http://jackherrington.com*.

Emily Kim is the co-founder and managing partner of the company Trilemetry, Inc., which specializes in software design, programming, and education.

Acknowledgments and Dedication

I'd like to acknowledge the help of Mike Potter at Adobe in the inspiration, design, and writing of this book. My thanks to Jen Blackledge for doing the technical review on the manuscript. A big thank you to my editor, Audrey Doyle, who is as astute with her comments as she is deft with her editing touch.

This book is dedicated to my beautiful wife, Lori, and awesome daughter, Megan. They are both the reason and the inspiration for this book.

—Jack Herrington

Publisher's Acknowledgments

O'Reilly and Adobe extend deepest thanks to Emily Kim and the entire team at Trilemetry (*www.trilemetry.com*). The learning materials that inspired this book were created for Adobe by Trilemetry as an online resource. You can find this material at *http://learn.adobe.com/wiki/display/Flex/Getting+Started*. The scope of the materials online is quite wide in contrast to what you'll find in this book, and we heartily recommend you use both as learning resources as you develop your Flex skills.

CHAPTER 1

Installing Flex Builder 3

Getting started with Flex begins with downloading the Flex Builder 3 integrated development environment (IDE). You can do that for free by going to the Adobe website (*http://adobe.com/flex*) and clicking on the Try Flex Builder 3 link. It's a pretty big download, so while you are waiting you might want to check out Chapter 2 to get some inspiration regarding what you can do with Flex.

Installing the IDE

Flex Builder installs just like any other software you would install on your Windows, Macintosh, or Linux box. The only small difference is that you will need to close your browser(s) so that the installer can upgrade your version of Flash Player to the debugger version. You will want to do that so that you can use the full debugging capabilities built into Flex Builder 3. The debugging system is very good, and becoming familiar with it will be well worth your time.

I strongly suggest that when the download page prompts you to subscribe to the email notifications from Adobe you accept the offer. It's a spam-free mailing list that gives you news and information about Flex and comes in handy as you delve deeper into the framework.

Figure 1-1. The startup splash screen

Once you have the software installed, launch it and you should see the splash screen shown in Figure 1-1.

On the splash screen you will see the words *Built on Eclipse*. Eclipse is an extensible cross-platform IDE developed by IBM that is popular in the Java™ world. However, you can also use it to build PHP as well as Rails or, in this case, Flex applications.

If you are familiar with Eclipse you will be fairly familiar with what you see in Figure 1-2.

Figure 1-2 shows the IDE when no projects are defined. On the upper left is the project and file area. On the bottom left is the Outline inspector that will show you the nested tags in your Flex application files. On the top right is the Start page that comes up by default. You should check out the links on the Start page because they will bring you to helpful material to get you started. The bottom-right panel, labeled Problems, is where you are alerted to issues (e.g., syntax errors) in your Flex code that keep Flex Builder from successfully compiling your application.

Having Some Image Fun

To get started quickly with Flex, select a new Flex project from the New item in the File menu. Use whatever project name you like. I used "starter." From there, take any image from your

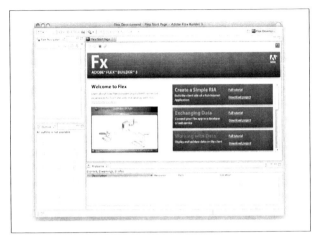

Figure 1-2. The empty Start page

computer, rename it to *myimage.jpg*, and drop it into the *src* folder of your new project.

Next, double-click on the MXML file for the application and add the code in Example 1-1.

Example 1-1. Starter.mxml

```
<?xml version="1.0" encoding="utf-8"?>
<mx:Application xmlns:mx="http://www.adobe.com/2006/mxml"
  layout="absolute">
  <mx:Image source="@Embed('mypicture.jpg')" height="100"
    top="30"
left="30" rotation="-10">
    <mx:filters>
      <mx:DropShadowFilter />
    </mx:filters>
  </mx:Image>
</mx:Application>
```

Now use the Run command in the Run menu to run the application. You should see your picture rotated a little bit, with a drop shadow added. Already, you can see that Flex can do some things that are difficult to do in the browser without any code.

Our next step will be to add some dynamic behavior to the example by adding controls for the rotation, the sizing, and the visibility of the image. The updated code appears in Example 1-2.

Example 1-2. Starter.mxml updated with controls

```
<?xml version="1.0" encoding="utf-8"?>
<mx:Application xmlns:mx="http://www.adobe.com/2006/mxml"
  layout="absolute">
  <mx:HBox top="10" left="10">
    <mx:HSlider minimum="-30" maximum="30" value="-10"
      toolTip="Rotation"
      change="myimg.rotation=event.currentTarget.value"
        liveDragging="true" />
    <mx:HSlider minimum="100" maximum="300" value="100"
      toolTip="Size"
      change="myimg.height=event.currentTarget.value"
        liveDragging="true" />
    <mx:CheckBox label="Visible" change="myimg.visible=
      event.currentTarget.selected"
      selected="true"/>
  </mx:HBox>
  <mx:Image id="myimg" source="@Embed('mypicture.jpg')"
    height="100" top="60" left="30" rotation="-10">
    <mx:filters>
      <mx:DropShadowFilter />
    </mx:filters>
  </mx:Image>
</mx:Application>
```

Now we have two sliders and a checkbox. One slider controls the rotation and the other controls the size of the image as the user adjusts the setting. The checkbox will hide or show the image. Figure 1-3 shows the result.

To have a little more fun with the example I'll add some effects that fade the image in or out when its shown or hidden. Example 1-3 shows the updated image code.

Figure 1-3. Our starter application so far

Example 1-3. The updated image code

```
<mx:Image id="myimg" source="@Embed('mypicture.jpg')"
  height="100" top="60" left="30" rotation="-10">
    <mx:filters>
      <mx:DropShadowFilter />
    </mx:filters>
    <mx:showEffect>
      <mx:Fade alphaFrom="0" alphaTo="1" duration="1000" />
    </mx:showEffect>
    <mx:hideEffect>
      <mx:Fade alphaFrom="1" alphaTo="0" duration="1000" />
    </mx:hideEffect>
  </mx:Image>
```

I've chosen to use a fade effect, but there are lots of different filters and effects that you can apply to any Flex control. You can even combine effects in parallel or as a sequence to create cool transitions almost always without using any ActionScript code.

CHAPTER 2

Flex in Action

Flash has always been a great tool for adding interactivity to a website. But with the advent of Flex a whole new group of engineers, designers, and enthusiasts have been able to build a wide variety of Flash applications. This chapter will discuss a cross section of applications to give you some ideas for what you can do with Flex. As you are looking through these examples, bear two things in mind:

- Although these examples often look dauntingly complex to implement, the Flex framework makes much of this work very easy.

- All of these applications work without any changes on Windows, Macintosh, and Linux, both in the browser and, often, on the desktop using Adobe's AIR technology.

I found most of the examples in this chapter in the Flex Showcase portion of the Flex.org (*http://flex.org*) website (*http://flex.org/*). The Showcase has an RSS feed that is worth subscribing to so that you can get a sense of what other people are producing using Flex.

E-Commerce

When your products are beautiful you want a beautiful way to present them to your customers. With that in mind, check out the Voelkl (*http://www.voelkl-snowboards.com*) snowboard se-

Figure 2-1. Choose your weapon!

lector in Figure 2-1. At the top of the page you can hover your mouse pointer over each snowboard design to find out more about it, as well as filter the selection of boards to just those for men, women, or rookies/kids.

Choose your weapon indeed, my friend! This site also demonstrates how Flex applications can seamlessly integrate with HTML pages. Flex does not need to take up the entire page. You can use Flex to build any size page element you want. And you can have the Flex application talk back to the JavaScript on the page to further link the Flash application with the HTML.

One of the most well-known Flash applications is the MINI car Configurator (*http://miniusa.com/?#/build/configurator/ mini_conv-m*) shown in Figure 2-2.

This astounding Flash application will walk you through configuring a MINI Cooper both inside and out. It's inviting, fun, and thoroughly engaging. It certainly makes me want to buy a MINI.

When you try out the MINI Configurator, which I hope you do, don't be taken aback by the complexity of the interface.

Figure 2-2. The MINI Configurator

The controls, event model, and CSS skinning in Flex make it easy to build complex interfaces that are easy to understand and maintain at the ActionScript level.

Online Applications

It seems like every month another company comes out with a web version of an application that used to be available only on the desktop. Sure, it's nice to be able to use an application without having to download and install it. However, I don't know about you, but I don't find them all that good. Well, I didn't, until I saw SlideRocket (*http://www.sliderocket.com/*), a Flex-based version of a slide show editor and presenter.

As you can see in Figure 2-3, the editor portion of the interface is both full-featured and elegant.

Figure 2-3. SlideRocket's editor screen

SlideRocket is one of the most amazing applications I've seen on any platform in years. It's well worth your time to check it out.

Another company doing some innovative application work is Aviary (*http://a.viary.com*). Shown in Figure 2-4 is Aviary's on-line image editing application that is written in Flex.

Figure 2-4. Aviary's image editor

Figure 2-5. The online version of Photoshop Elements

This application shows not only the functionality and elegance that you can achieve in Flex interfaces, but also the speed of the Flash Player in executing image manipulation functions.

Adobe itself is making use of Flex to build an online suite of applications. Shown in Figure 2-5 is the online version of Photoshop Elements built completely in Flex.

Another impressive online application is Adobe's Buzzword project (*http://buzzword.acrobat.com/*), shown in Figure 2-6.

Not only is it beautifully designed, but it's also fast, works anywhere, and can be used in conjunction with other contributors. Adobe developed Buzzword in Flex.

Multimedia

Of course, what catalog of Flash applications would be complete without a movie viewer? I don't want to show you the usual YouTube thing, so I'll show you video integrated with e-commerce to sell robots for a company called RobotWorx

Figure 2-6. The Buzzword Editor

(*http://www.robots.com/movies.php?tag=40*). Figure 2-7 shows
the RobotWorx page with the embedded custom video player.

The Flex application is seamlessly embedded within the larger
HTML page. The videos available for the particular robot are
shown along the bottom in the style of YouTube. The video of
the robot (doing some arc welding in this case) is shown on the
left. And a static image of the robot is shown on the right.

Plug-ins and Widgets

You can also use Flex to implement the plug-ins and widgets
that go on sites such as Facebook. Shown in Figure 2-8 is a
Flex-based node graph, called SocioGraph (*http://apps.face
book.com/sociograph/*), which displays the connections between you and your Facebook friends. It's an easy add-in
application to your Facebook account.

I admit that I don't have a lot of Facebook friends; your graph
is probably a lot busier than mine is. But as I click around the

Figure 2-7. The RobotWorx custom movie player

nodes more friends pop out and I get a better feel for how I am connected to people simply by interacting with this control. Even with my sparse set of data there is a lot of fun to be had.

You can also use Flex to host a set of widgets as a portal. YourMinis (*http://www.yourminis.com/start*), shown in Figure 2-9, does a great job of presenting customizable portals that look great and work well.

Figure 2-8. SocioGraph Facebook plug-in

Figure 2-9. The YourMinis portal built into Flex

You can have multiple pages in your portal. And you can even place a YourMinis widget on any regular HTML page as a standalone piece. This makes YourMinis not only a great portal, but also a great place to build widgets that can go anywhere.

Dashboards

Controlling a business is one thing, but how about controlling devices—such as a yacht, for example? Yes, Flex has done that too. Have a look at Figure 2-10 to see the InteliSea yacht alarm, monitoring, and control system (*http://www.inteli sea.com/demo/demo.htm*).

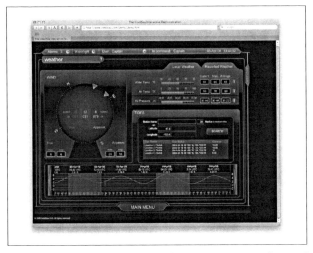

Figure 2-10. The InteliSea yacht alarm, monitoring, and control system

It makes me want to go out and buy a yacht just so that I can play with this thing. Of course, there is the expense of the yacht. Hmmm... Oh, well. I wonder if I can get this trimmed down to work on radio-controlled boats.

ILOG Visualization Products has developed a graphing dashboard based on the CIA World FactBook, which comprises

U.S. government profiles of countries and territories around the world. This is shown in Figure 2-11.

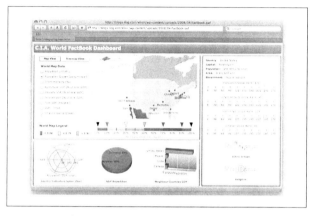

Figure 2-11. The CIA World FactBook viewer

This shows a nice combination of the controls available in the ILOG Elixir toolkit, including 2D and 3D charts, a tree view, interactive maps, and more. For more information on the ILOG Elixir toolkit, visit *http://www.ilog.com/products/elixir/*. I also discuss ILOG Elixir in more detail in Chapter 7.

Desktop Applications

Not only is Flex good for making great web applications, but you also can use it to build desktop applications using exactly the same Flex toolkit. To demonstrate I'll show two desktop applications. The first is a chat application, shown in Figure 2-12. The application is called Pownce (*http://pownce.com/*) and it sits on the desktop using Adobe's AIR technology.

Figure 2-12. The Pownce chat client

I can tell you from experience that building this type of chat application in Ajax is a real hassle. Cross-domain security becomes an issue that requires that you proxy all of the requests. And making lots of HTTP requests can create memory leaks on some browsers that will leave you banging your head against the wall trying to fix all of the bugs that may or may not appear at any given time. Flex gets around these hassles by sitting on top of the robust and cross-platform Flash Player.

Another excellent example of an online application is the AIR-based eBay Desktop (*http://desktop.ebay.com*), shown in Figure 2-13.

Figure 2-13. The eBay Desktop application

From here, you can browse what is available for sale, bid on items, watch your auctions, and so on. And it even maintains the native look and feel of the operating system.

What Will You Do?

The chapters that follow will show you the parts and pieces that were used to create all of these applications. But it's up to you to find the inspiration and creativity to take your applications to the next level. Thankfully, with Flex you will have all the tools you need to take you there.

CHAPTER 3

Flex 101: Step by Step

This chapter will walk you step by step through the process of constructing a Flex application. That starts with learning how Flex works. Flex is an XML-based language that is compiled into Flash applications. You can see the process portrayed graphically in Figure 3-1.

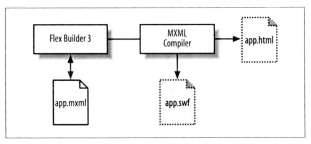

Figure 3-1. The flow of Flex application building

Going from the bottom left of Figure 3-1 to the top right, Flex Builder 3 helps you write *app.mxml*, the Flex application. That in turn is run through the MXML compiler that generates a SWF file for the application. It also generates a temporary HTML test page that hosts the SWF so that you can test it. The SWF and the HTML are replaced after each compile, so I made them dashed to indicate that they are temporary.

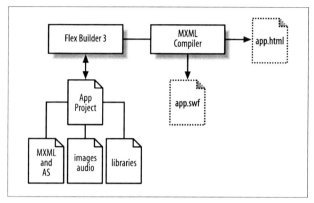

Figure 3-2. The Flex project creating a single SWF

Flex Builder is actually a bit more useful than this in that it really manages *projects*, which are sets of Flex applications and components, as well as assets (e.g., images and audio that are embedded in the SWF) and any libraries that your project references. This is shown in Figure 3-2.

Now that you have a general idea of how Flex Builder 3 creates Flex applications, it's time to walk through the process of creating a real Flex application.

A Flickr Viewer

The final sample application in this chapter is a Flickr image viewer. The end result looks like Figure 3-3.

With this application, you can type a search term into the text box, click the Search button, and see the result in the list view.

This example is a bit more complex than the example in Chapter 1, so I'll walk you through building it in Flex Builder.

The first step is to create a new Flex application project named FlickrRIA, which you can do by following these steps:

Figure 3-3. The Flickr viewer

1. In the Flex Builder IDE, select File→New→Flex Project and name the project FlickrRIA.

2. Accept the default location for the project and confirm that the Application Type is Web Application and that the Server Technology is set to None.

3. Click Finish to create the project.

The *FlickrRIA.mxml* application file opens in the MXML editor. The editor is in Source mode. Now, you need to format the display. To do so, follow these steps:

1. In the opening `Application` tag, delete the code `layout="absolute"`.

2. For the `Application` tag, add a `backgroundGradientColors` attribute with a value of `[0xFFFFFF, 0xAAAAAA]`, a `horizontalAlign` attribute with a value of `left`, a `verticalGap` attribute with a value of `15`, and a `horizontalGap` attribute with a value of `15`.

   Example 3-1 shows the code for the `Application` tag.

Example 3-1. The Application tag

```
<mx:Application xmlns:mx="http://www.adobe.com
  /2006/mxml"
    backgroundGradientColors="[0xFFFFFF,0xAAAAAA]"
    horizontalAlign="left"
    verticalGap="15" horizontalGap="15" >
```

Next, we'll lay out the search form in Design mode:

1. Click the Design button to change to Design mode. Using Design mode is the easiest way to lay out a form in Flex Builder.

2. From the Components view, drag an HBox component from the *Layout* folder to the design area. Keep the default values of the component. The HBox component contains the label, input field, and button for the form and displays them horizontally.

NOTE

The blue lines that appear in the design area help you position the component. When you release the component in the design area, it snaps into position.

---

3. Drag the Label component from the *Controls* folder to the HBox component.

4. To change the default appearance of the Label component, double-click the Label component and type in the Flickr tags or terms that you want to search (see Figure 3-4).

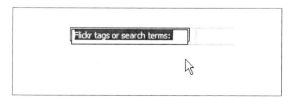

Figure 3-4. The search label

---

5. Drag the `TextInput` component from the *Controls* folder to the position following the `Label` component in the `HBox`. The `TextInput` component provides the user with a space to input search terms (see Figure 3-5).

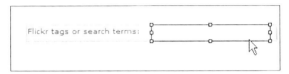

Figure 3-5. The TextInput field

6. Drag a `Button` component from the *Controls* folder to the position following the `TextInput` component in the `HBox` component.

7. Double-click the `Button` component and enter **Search** to change the default appearance.

At this point, we need to create the `HTTPService` object:

1. Change to Source mode.

2. Use the `HTTPService` component to call the Flickr service and return the results. After the opening `Application` tag and before the `HBox` component, create an `HTTPService` component, but do not give it a closing tag.

3. To the `HTTPService` component, add an `id` attribute with a value of **photoService**, a `url` attribute with a value of *http://api.flickr.com/services/feeds/photos_public.gne*, and a `result` attribute with a value of **photoHan dler(event)**. The `photoHandler` event packages the service results. We will create the {{`photoHandler`}} function later.

Example 3-2 shows the relevant code.

Example 3-2. The HTTPService control

```
<mx:HTTPService id="photoService"

        url="http://api.flickr.com/services/feeds
```

```
                /photos_public.gne"
            result="photoHandler(event)"/>
```

Now it's time to create a bindable XML variable in ActionScript 3.0. To do so, follow these steps:

1. Before the `HTTPService` component, add a `Script` component by typing `<mx:Script>`. Flex Builder completes the tag for you. Alternatively, you can place the `Script` component after the `HTTPService` component, as shown in Example 3-3.

   Example 3-3. The blank script tag

   ```
   <mx:Script>
   <![CDATA[
   ]]>
   </mx:Script>
   ```

2. In the `mx:Script` block, enter `import mx.collections.ArrayCollection`. `ArrayCollection` is the type of object that is used as a data provider.

   The relevant code is shown in Example 3-4.

   Example 3-4. The first import statement

   ```
   <mx:Script>
   <![CDATA[
       import mx.collections.ArrayCollection;
   ]]>
   </mx:Script>
   ```

3. After the `ArrayCollection` import statement, enter `import mx.rpc.events.ResultEvent` to import the `ResultEvent` class. The `ResultEvent` class is the type of event that the `HTTPService` generates. You can see this in Example 3-5.

   Example 3-5. The second import statement

   ```
   <mx:Script>
   <![CDATA[
       import mx.collections.ArrayCollection;
       import mx.rpc.events.ResultEvent;
   ]]>
   </mx:Script>
   ```

4. Create a **bindable** private variable named **photoFeed** of the **ArrayCollection** class after the import statement in the **mx:Script** block. The **photoFeed ArrayCollection** is populated with the **HTTPService** response data. Example 3-6 shows the completed script.

Example 3-6. The completed script

```
<mx:Script>
<![CDATA[
    import mx.collections.ArrayCollection;
    import mx.rpc.events.ResultEvent;

    [Bindable]
    private var photoFeed:ArrayCollection;
]]>
</mx:Script>
```

With the bindable XML variable created, it's time to create the Submit button click handler, and send the **HTTPService** request and keywords to the Flickr API:

1. Using the Outline view, locate the **Button** component in the **HBox** component. Clicking the **Button** component in the Outline view locates the **Button** component code in Source mode. This is shown in Figure 3-6.

Figure 3-6. The Button component in the Outline view

2. To the **Button** component, add a **click** attribute with a value of **requestPhotos()**:

```
<mx:Button label="Search" click="requestPhotos()"/>
```

When a user clicks the button, it calls the **requestPhotos()** handler, which initiates the **HTTPService** call.

3. Using the Outline view, locate the `TextInput` component in the `HBox` component and add an `id` attribute with a value of `searchTerms`. The instance name for the `TextInput` component is `id`, as shown here:

```
<mx:TextInput id="searchTerms"/>
```

4. In the `mx:Script` block, create a private function named `requestPhotos()` with a return value of `*void`. This is the function where the `HTTPService` call is initiated.

The relevant code appears in Example 3-7.

Example 3-7. The requestPhotos method

```
<mx:Script>
<![CDATA[
    import mx.collections.ArrayCollection;
    import mx.rpc.events.ResultEvent;

    [Bindable]
    private var photoFeed:ArrayCollection;
    private function requestPhotos():void{
    }
]]>
</mx:Script>
```

5. In the function, cancel any previous requests to `photoService` by using the `cancel` method. The instance name of the `HTTPService` component is `photoService`.

6. Create an `Object` variable named `params`.

7. Create a format parameter of the `params` variable with a value of `rss_200_enc`. This value tells Flickr how to package the response.

8. Create a `tags` parameter of the `params` variable with a value of `searchTerms.text`. This is the value that was entered in the search field.

9. Send the request and `params` variable to Flickr by using the `send` method of `photoService`. Example 3-8 shows the complete function.

Example 3-8. The complete requestPhotos function

```
<mx:Script>
<![CDATA[
    import mx.collections.ArrayCollection;
    import mx.rpc.events.ResultEvent;

    [Bindable]
    private var photoFeed:ArrayCollection;

    private function requestPhotos():void{
        photoService.cancel();
        var params:Object = new Object();
        params.format = 'rss_200_enc';
        params.tags = searchTerms.text;
        photoService.send(params);
    }
]]>
</mx:Script>
```

Now it's time to create the HTTPService result handler and to populate the photoFeed XML variable:

1. After the requestPhotos() function, create a private function named photoHandler and pass an event of type ResultEvent to the function. The return type is void. The photoHandler handles the response from the HTTPSer vice call. At this point, your code should look like Example 3-9.

Example 3-9. The complete script block

```
<mx:Script>
<![CDATA[
    import mx.collections.ArrayCollection;
    import mx.rpc.events.ResultEvent;

    [Bindable]
    private var photoFeed:ArrayCollection;

    private function requestPhotos():void{
        photoService.cancel();
        var params:Object = new Object();
        params.format = 'rss_200_enc';
        params.tags = searchTerms.text;
        photoService.send(params);
```

```
        }
        private function photoHandler(event:ResultEvent)
          :void{
        }
   ]]>
   </mx:Script>
```

2. In the photoHandler() function, populate the photoFeed
   variable with the data located in the event object,
   event.result.rss.channel.item, and type it as ArrayCol
   lection. Your code should now look like Example 3-10.

   Example 3-10. Adding the photoHandler

```
<mx:Script>
<![CDATA[
    import mx.collections.ArrayCollection;
    import mx.rpc.events.ResultEvent;

    [Bindable]
    private var photoFeed:ArrayCollection;

    private function requestPhotos():void{
        photoService.cancel();
        var params:Object = new Object();
        params.format = 'rss_200_enc';
        params.tags = searchTerms.text;
        photoService.send(params);
    }

    private function photoHandler(event:ResultEvent)
      :void{
        photoFeed = event.result.rss.channel.item as
          ArrayCollection;
    }
]]>
</mx:Script>
```

Now we're ready to create the Tile component in MXML, bind
the photoFeed XML data to the TileList component, and then
create the thumbnails item renderer in the Tile component:

1. We will use a TileList component to display the images.
   After the HBox component and before the closing Appli
   cation tag, add a TileList component with a width of

100% and a `height` of 100%. This `TileList` is shown in Example 3-11.

Example 3-11. The TileList

```
<mx:TileList width="100%" height="100%">
</mx:TileList>
```

2. Using the Outline view, locate the `TileList` component and add an attribute of `dataProvider` with a value of `{photoFeed}` to bind the data to the tile component. (Remember to move the `>` to the end of the `dataProvider` line.) Example 3-12 shows the completed `TileList` component.

Example 3-12. The completed TileList

```
<mx:TileList width="100%" height="100%"
    dataProvider="{photoFeed}">
</mx:TileList>
```

3. The item renderer renders the layout for each item in the `TileList`. Within the `TileList` component, add an `item Renderer` property, using the code shown in Example 3-13.

Example 3-13. The itemRenderer attribute

```
<mx:TileList width="100%" height="100%"
    dataProvider="{photoFeed}">
    <mx:itemRenderer>
    </mx:itemRenderer>
</mx:TileList>
```

4. Now we'll create a layout component for the item renderer. Within the `itemRenderer` property, add a `Compo nent` component using the code shown in Example 3-14.

Example 3-14. Adding the Component

```
<mx:TileList width="100%" height="100%"
    dataProvider="{photoFeed}">
    <mx:itemRenderer>
        <mx:Component>
        </mx:Component>
```

```
        </mx:itemRenderer>
    </mx:TileList>
```

5. To create the layout the item renderer will use, within
   the Component add the VBox component with a width attribute with a value of 125 and a height attribute with a
   value of 125. Add paddingBottom, paddingLeft, padding
   Top, and paddingRight attributes each with a value of 5.
   The code is shown in Example 3-15.

Example 3-15. Adding the VBox

```
<mx:TileList width="100%" height="100%"
    dataProvider="{photoFeed}">
    <mx:itemRenderer>
        <mx:Component>
            <mx:VBox width="125" height="125"
                paddingBottom="5"
                paddingLeft="5"
                paddingTop="5"
                paddingRight="5">
            </mx:VBox>
        </mx:Component>
    </mx:itemRenderer>
</mx:TileList>
```

6. Within the VBox component, create an Image component.
   Add a width attribute with a value of 75 and a height
   attribute with a value of 75. The itemRenderer passes
   values to the Image component through the Image component's data property. Add a source with a value of
   {data.thumbnail.url} to the Image component to populate the image. The code is shown in Example 3-16.

Example 3-16. Adding the Image tag

```
<mx:TileList width="100%" height="100%"
    dataProvider="{photoFeed}">
    <mx:itemRenderer>
        <mx:Component>
            <mx:VBox width="125" height="125"
                paddingBottom="5"
                paddingLeft="5"
                paddingTop="5"
                paddingRight="5">
                <mx:Image width="75" height="75"
```

```
                    source="{data.thumbnail.url}"/>
            </mx:VBox>
        </mx:Component>
    </mx:itemRenderer>
</mx:TileList>
```

7. After the `Image` component, create a `Text` component
   with the `text` attribute having a value of `{data.credit}`
   to display the name of the photographer. The code is
   shown in Example 3-17.

Example 3-17. Adding the Text component

```
<mx:TileList width="100%" height="100%"
    dataProvider="{photoFeed}">
    <mx:itemRenderer>
        <mx:Component>
            <mx:VBox width="125" height="125"
                paddingBottom="5"
                paddingLeft="5"
                paddingTop="5"
                paddingRight="5">
                <mx:Image width="75" height="75"
                    source="{data.thumbnail.url}"/>
                <mx:Text text="{data.credit}"/>
            </mx:VBox>
        </mx:Component>
    </mx:itemRenderer>
</mx:TileList>
```

8. Save and then run the application. You should see a
   form. In the form, submit a search term and you should
   see the application display the relevant image(s).

At this point, you should be ready to separate the thumbnail
display into a custom component:

1. Create a new component by selecting
   File→New→MXML Component. The filename for this is
   FlickrThumbnail and the component should be based on
   `VBox`. Set the `width` to 125 and the `height` to 125.

2. Using the Outline view, locate the `TileList` component.

3. Cut the `Image` and `Text` components from the `VBox` component in `TileList`, and paste them into *FlickrThumb
   nail.mxml*. This starting code is shown in Example 3-18.

Example 3-18. The new FlickrThumbnail.mxml

```
<?xml version="1.0" encoding="utf-8"?>
<mx:VBox xmlns:mx="http://www.adobe.com/2006/mxml"
    width="125" height="125">
        <mx:Image width="75" height="75"
            source="{data.thumbnail.url}"/>
        <mx:Text text="{data.credit}"/>
</mx:VBox>
```

4. Add the following attributes to the VBox component: paddingBottom, paddingTop, paddingRight, and paddin gLeft, each with a value of 5; horizontalScrollPolicy and verticalScrollPolicy, both with a value of off; and horizontalAlign with a value of center. The updated code is shown in Example 3-19.

Example 3-19. Updating the VBox component source

```
<?xml version="1.0" encoding="utf-8"?>
<mx:VBox xmlns:mx="http://www.adobe.com/2006/mxml"
    width="125" height="125"
    paddingBottom="5" paddingLeft="5" paddingTop="5"
      paddingRight="5"
    horizontalScrollPolicy="off" verticalScrollPolicy=
      "off"
    horizontalAlign="center">
        <mx:Image width="75" height="75"
            source="{data.thumbnail.url}"/>
        <mx:Text text="{data.credit}"/>
</mx:VBox>
```

5. Using the Outline view, locate the TileList component in the *FlickrRIA.mxml* template.

6. Delete the code for the itemRenderer, Component, and VBox components.

7. Add the attribute itemRenderer to the TileList component with a value of FlickrThumbnail. The completed code is shown in Example 3-20.

Example 3-20. Referencing the itemRenderer

```
<mx:TileList width="100%" height="100%"
        dataProvider="{photoFeed}"
```

```
                     itemRenderer="FlickrThumbnail">
      </mx:TileList>
```

8. Compile and run the application.

At this point, you should see something very similar to what you had when you created the inline component `itemRenderer`.

The final code for *FlickrRIA.mxml* is shown in Example 3-21.

Example 3-21. FlickrRIA.mxml

```
<?xml version="1.0" encoding="utf-8"?>
<mx:Application xmlns:mx="http://www.adobe.com/2006/mxml"
    backgroundGradientColors="[0xFFFFFF, 0xAAAAAA]"
    horizontalAlign="left"
    verticalGap="15"
    horizontalGap="15">
    <mx:Script>
        <![CDATA[
            import mx.collections.ArrayCollection;
            import mx.rpc.events.ResultEvent;

            [Bindable]
            private var photoFeed:ArrayCollection;
            private function requestPhotos():void {
                photoService.cancel();
                var params:Object = new Object();
                params.format = 'rss_200_enc';
                params.tags = searchTerms.text;
                photoService.send(params);
            }
            private function photoHandler(event:ResultEvent)
              :void {
                photoFeed = event.result.rss.channel.item as
                    ArrayCollection;
            }
        ]]>
    </mx:Script>
    <mx:HTTPService id="photoService"

        url="http://api.flickr.com/services/feeds
          /photos_public.gne"
        result="photoHandler(event)" />
    <mx:HBox>
        <mx:Label text="Flickr tags or search terms:" />
        <mx:TextInput id="searchTerms" />
        <mx:Button label="Search"
```

```
                    click="requestPhotos()" />
    </mx:HBox>
    <mx:TileList width="100%" height="100%"
        dataProvider="{photoFeed}"
        itemRenderer="FlickrThumbnail">
    </mx:TileList>
</mx:Application>
```

The complete code for the image item rendering component is shown in Example 3-22.

Example 3-22. The custom image rendering component

```
<?xml version="1.0" encoding="utf-8"?>
<mx:VBox xmlns:mx="http://www.adobe.com/2006/mxml"
    width="125" height="125"
    horizontalAlign="center"
    paddingBottom="5" paddingLeft="5" paddingRight="5"
      paddingTop="5">
    <mx:Image
        width="75" height="75"
        source="{data.thumbnail.url}" />
    <mx:Text width="100" text="{data.credit}" />
</mx:VBox>
```

As you can see from this example, it is very easy to access web services from Flex. It's also easy to parse their contents using the E4X syntax built directly into ActionScript 3, which makes querying XML data as easy as using standard dot notation. It's nice to wrap the whole thing up with a display using a list of images managed by `TileList` with a custom `itemRenderer`.

CHAPTER 4

Flex Controls and Layout

The first step in building a Flex application is to create the user interface. Flex not only has a rich set of controls. It also has a complete set of layout mechanisms that make it easy to build user interfaces that look good and can scale appropriately as the display area of the Flash application is resized.

This chapter covers both layout mechanisms and controls. We will start by covering the layout mechanisms, and then we will discuss the available controls.

The Application Container

At the root of a Flex application is a single container, called the `Application` container, which holds all other containers and components. The `Application` container lays out all its children vertically by default (when the `layout` property is not specifically defined). There are three possible values for the `Application` component's `layout` property:

vertical

> Lays out each child component vertically from the top of the application to the bottom in the specified order

horizontal

> Lays out each child component horizontally from the left of the application to the right in the specified order

Figure 4-1. Controls using the Application container

absolute

Does no automatic layout, and requires you to explicitly define the location of each child component

If the `Application` component's layout property is `absolute`, each child component must have an *x* and *y* coordinate defined; otherwise, the component will be displayed in the (0,0) position.

The `Application` container can also be formatted using any of the several style parameters that are available, including `back groundGradientColors` and `verticalGap`. In Example 4-1, the `Application` tag is used to lay out the child controls.

Example 4-1. The Application MXML

```
<?xml version="1.0" encoding="utf-8"?>
<mx:Application xmlns:mx="http://www.adobe.com/2006/mxml"
 backgroundGradientColors="[#FFFFFF, #FFDE00]" verticalGap="15"
 layout="horizontal">
 <mx:Image source="assets/animals03.jpg" />
 <mx:Label text="Photographed by Elsie Weil" fontSize="15"
   fontWeight="bold" />
</mx:Application>
```

Figure 4-1 shows the result of this code.

The Box Class

The Box class is the base class for the VBox and HBox classes:

- The VBox container renders all child display objects vertically.
- The HBox container renders all child display objects horizontally.

The Application object behaves like a VBox by default (vertical layout), but you can also set it to use absolute or horizontal layout.

VBox and HBox flow like HTML, only in one direction.

Example 4-2 shows the default layout method used by the VBox container (vertical).

Example 4-2. Using the VBox container

```
<?xml version="1.0" encoding="utf-8"?>
<mx:Application xmlns:mx="http://www.adobe.com/2006/mxml"
 backgroundColor="#FFFFFF" backgroundAlpha="0">
 <mx:VBox>
  <mx:Button label="&lt; prev" left="10" top="120" />
  <mx:Image source="assets/animals03.jpg" horizontalCenter="0"
    top="30"/>
  <mx:Label text="Photographed by Elsie Weil"
    horizontalCenter="0" top="250"/>
  <mx:Button label="next &gt;" right="10" top="120"/>
 </mx:VBox>
</mx:Application>
```

Figure 4-2 shows the result of this code.

Figure 4-2. A VBox layout

Example 4-3 shows the default layout method used by the HBox container (horizontal).

Example 4-3. Using the HBox container

```
<?xml version="1.0" encoding="utf-8"?>
<mx:Application xmlns:mx="http://www.adobe.com/2006/mxml"
 backgroundColor="#FFFFFF" backgroundAlpha="0">
 <mx:HBox>
  <mx:Button label="&lt; prev" left="10" top="120" />
  <mx:Image source="assets/animals03.jpg" horizontalCenter="0"
    top="30"/>
  <mx:Label text="Photographed by Elsie Weil"
    horizontalCenter="0" top="250"/>
  <mx:Button label="next &gt;" right="10" top="120"/>
 </mx:HBox>
</mx:Application>
```

Figure 4-3 shows the result.

You can also use both VBox and HBox to achieve a desired layout. For instance, Example 4-4 nests an HBox inside a VBox, demon-

Figure 4-3. An HBox layout

strating that container controls can have other containers as children.

Example 4-4. Using both the VBox and the HBox containers

```
<?xml version="1.0" encoding="utf-8"?>
<mx:Application xmlns:mx="http://www.adobe.com/2006/mxml"
 backgroundColor="#FFFFFF" backgroundAlpha="0">
 <mx:VBox horizontalAlign="center" verticalGap="15">
   <mx:HBox verticalAlign="middle" horizontalGap="15">
     <mx:Button label="&lt; prev" left="10" top="120" />
     <mx:Image source="assets/animals03.jpg"
       horizontalCenter="0" top="30"/>
     <mx:Button label="next &gt;" right="10" top="120"/>
   </mx:HBox>
   <mx:Label text="Photographed by Elsie Weil"
     horizontalCenter="0" top="250"/>
 </mx:VBox>
</mx:Application>
```

Figure 4-4 shows the result of Example 4-4.

The Canvas Container (Absolute Positioning)

Canvas is the only container that lets you explicitly specify the location of its children within the container. The Canvas object has only one layout value: absolute. You can use the x and y properties of child components for pixel-perfect layouts. If the display window is resized, the child components stay fixed in place and may appear cut off. Using absolute positioning you can make child controls overlap if desired.

Figure 4-4. A combination VBox and HBox layout

Example 4-5 is some sample code for an absolutely positioned layout.

Example 4-5. An absolutely positioned layout

```
<?xml version="1.0" encoding="utf-8"?>
<mx:Application xmlns:mx="http://www.adobe.com/2006/mxml"
 layout="absolute" backgroundColor="#FFFFFF"
   backgroundAlpha="0">
 <mx:Canvas x="23" y="34">
  <mx:Button label="&lt; prev" x="4" y="97" />
  <mx:Image source="assets/animals03.jpg" x="85" y="4" />
  <mx:Label text="Photographed by Elsie Weil" x="85"
    y="230" />
  <mx:Button label="next &gt;" x="381" y="97" />
 </mx:Canvas>
</mx:Application>
```

Figure 4-5 shows the result.

The Canvas Container (Relative Positioning)

With relative positioning, also called constraint-based layout, you can anchor the sides or center of a component to positions which are relative to the component's container. The size and position of the components change when the user resizes the

Figure 4-5. An absolutely positioned image

application window. The container's `layout` property must be set to `absolute`. All constraints are set relative to the edges of the container, not to other controls in the container. The `left`, `right`, `top`, `bottom`, `horizontalCenter`, and `verticalCenter` properties are anchors in constraint-based layouts.

Example 4-6 shows the code for positioning children in a constraint-based layout using the `top`, `bottom`, `left`, `right`, `horizontalCenter`, and `verticalCenter` styles.

Example 4-6. Photo.mxml

```
<?xml version="1.0" encoding="utf-8"?>
<mx:Application xmlns:mx="http://www.adobe.com/2006/mxml"
 layout="absolute backgroundColor="#FFFFFF"
   backgroundAlpha="0">
 <mx:HDividedBox width="100%" height="300">
  <mx:Canvas backgroundColor="#FFFFCC" width="150"
    height="100%">
   <mx:Label text="Adjust this section" left="15" />
  </mx:Canvas>
  <mx:Canvas>
   <mx:Button label="&lt; prev" left="10" top="120"/>
   <mx:Image source="animals03.jpg" horizontalCenter="0"
     top="30"/>
   <mx:Label text="Photographed by Elsie Weil"
     horizontalCenter="0" top="250"/>
   <mx:Button label="next &gt;" right="10" top="120"/>
```

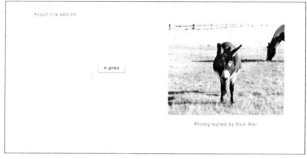

Figure 4-6. A constraint-based layout

```
   </mx:Canvas>
 </mx:HDividedBox>
</mx:Application>
```

When you launch this application you should see something similar to Figure 4-6.

You can adjust the size of the panel on the right by grabbing the control and moving the mouse to the left or right. This will move the image to match the size of the panel.

The Form Container

The Form container lets you control the layout of a form, mark form fields as required or, optionally, handle error messages, and bind your form data to the Flex data model to perform data checking and validation.

The Form container, like all containers, encapsulates and lays out its children. The Form container controls the size and layout of the contents of the form. The FormHeader defines a heading for your Form. Multiple FormHeading controls are allowed. A FormItem container specifies a Form element consisting of the following parts:

- A single label

- One or more child controls or containers, such as input controls

You can also insert other types of components into a **Form** container.

The code in Example 4-7 demonstrates use of a **Form** container control.

Example 4-7. CommentForm.mxml

```xml
<?xml version="1.0" encoding="utf-8"?>
<mx:Application xmlns:mx="http://www.adobe.com/2006/mxml"
 layout="absolute" backgroundColor="#FFFFFF"
   backgroundAlpha="0">
 <mx:Form x="50" y="50" verticalGap="15">
  <mx:FormHeading label="Send us comments" />
  <mx:FormItem label="Full Name:">
   <mx:TextInput id="fullName" />
  </mx:FormItem>
  <mx:FormItem label="Email:">
   <mx:TextInput id="email" />
  </mx:FormItem>
  <mx:FormItem label="Comments:">
   <mx:TextArea id="comments" />
  </mx:FormItem>
  <mx:FormItem>
   <mx:Button id="submit" label="submit" />
  </mx:FormItem>
  </mx:Form>
</mx:Application>
```

Figure 4-7 shows the result of this code.

Figure 4-7. A form-based layout

Combined Layouts

Containers can hold other containers. You can nest them to create sophisticated layouts, and you can create custom components that are made up of existing components. Example 4-8 shows an example of a complex nested layout. You should take care to use these container classes wisely and not to overuse them. Using too many nested containers can be the cause of performance problems in your application.

Example 4-8. A complex nested layout

```
<?xml version="1.0" encoding="utf-8"?>
<mx:Application xmlns:mx="http://www.adobe.com/2006/mxml"
 backgroundColor="#000000" layout="horizontal"
  horizontalGap="25">
 <mx:Style> Panel { backgroundAlpha: 1; borderAlpha: 1;
   headerColors: #c7c7c7, #ffffff;
   footerColors: #ffffff, #c7c7c7;
   paddingTop: 15; paddingRight: 15;
   paddingLeft: 15; paddingBottom: 15;
   shadowDirection: "right"; }
```

```
.header { color: #ffffff; fontSize: 15;
  fontWeight: "bold"; }</mx:Style>
<mx:VBox verticalGap="10">
 <mx:Panel title="Featured Photograph">
  <mx:Image source="assets/animals03.jpg" horizontalCenter="0"
    top="30" />
  <mx:Label text="Photographed by Elsie Weil"
    horizontalCenter="0" top="250" />
 </mx:Panel>
 <mx:Panel title="Provide feedback">
  <mx:Form x="50" y="50" verticalGap="15">
  <mx:FormHeading label="Send us comments" />
  <mx:FormItem label="Full Name:"><mx:TextInput
    id="fullName" />
  </mx:FormItem>
  <mx:FormItem label="Email:"><mx:TextInput id="email" />
  </mx:FormItem>
  <mx:FormItem label="Comments:"><mx:TextArea
    id="comments" />
  </mx:FormItem>
  <mx:FormItem><mx:Button id="submit" label="submit" />
  </mx:FormItem>
  </mx:Form>
 </mx:Panel>
</mx:VBox>
<mx:VBox verticalGap="25">
 <mx:Canvas>
  <mx:Label text="Category: Animals" styleName="header" />
  <mx:Image source="assets/animals03_sm.jpg" y="30" />
  <mx:Image source="assets/animals08_sm.jpg" y="120" />
  <mx:Image source="assets/animals09_sm.jpg" y="120"
    x="120" />
  <mx:Image source="assets/animals10_sm.jpg" y="120"
    x="240" />
  <mx:Image source="assets/animals11_sm.jpg" y="211" />
  <mx:Image source="assets/animals12_sm.jpg" y="211"
    x="120" />
  <mx:Image source="assets/animals06_sm.jpg" y="30"
    x="120" />
  <mx:Image source="assets/animals07_sm.jpg" y="30"
    x="240" />
 </mx:Canvas>
 <mx:Canvas>
  <mx:Label text="Category: Cities" styleName="header" />
  <mx:Image source="assets/city01_sm.jpg" y="30" />
  <mx:Image source="assets/city02_sm.jpg" y="30" x="120"/>
  <mx:Image source="assets/city03_sm.jpg" y="30" x="240" />
```

```
    <mx:Image source="assets/city04_sm.jpg" y="120" x="0" />
  </mx:Canvas>
 </mx:VBox>
</mx:Application>
```

Figure 4-8 shows the result of Example 4-8.

Figure 4-8. A complex layout using various types of layout mechanisms

The Panel Container

The Panel container consists of a title bar, a caption, a status message, a border, and a content area for its children. You can use Panel containers to wrap self-contained application modules. You can control the display layout by using the layout property set to **vertical** (the default), **horizontal**, or **absolute**. Each child must have its *x* and *y* positions set when using an absolute layout, or they must use anchors for a constraint-based layout.

Example 4-9 shows a sample Panel layout.

Example 4-9. Photo2.mxml

```
<?xml version="1.0" encoding="utf-8"?>
<mx:Application xmlns:mx="http://www.adobe.com/2006/mxml"
 backgroundGradientColors="[#FFFFFF, #000000]">
 <mx:Panel title="Featured Photograph"
  backgroundAlpha=".25" borderAlpha="1"
  headerColors="[#c7c7c7, #ffffff]"
  footerColors="[#ffffff, #c7c7c7]"
  paddingTop="15" paddingRight="15" paddingLeft="15"
    paddingBottom="15"
  shadowDirection="right">
   <mx:Image source="assets/animals03.jpg"
     horizontalCenter="0" top="30" />
   <mx:Label text="Photographed by Elsie Weil"
     horizontalCenter="0" top="250" />
 </mx:Panel>
</mx:Application>
```

Figure 4-9 shows this Panel-based layout.

Figure 4-9. A layout using the Panel container

In addition to panels, you also can use a `TitleWindow` class to provide windowing-style functionality. This can come in handy when you want to bring up an alert, or a modal dialog.

Controls

So many controls are available for you to use with Flex that it's almost hard to know where to begin. I suppose the best place to start is with the basic controls, such as labels, buttons, checkboxes, and so on. Example 4-10 shows an MXML application that provides a heaping helping of the basic control types.

Example 4-10. Buttons2.mxml

```
<?xml version="1.0" encoding="utf-8"?>
<mx:Application xmlns:mx="http://www.adobe.com/2006/mxml"
  layout="horizontal">
<mx:VBox horizontalAlign="left">
 <mx:Label text="Text label" />
 <mx:Label htmlText="&lt;b&gt;HTML&lt;/b&gt; text" />
 <mx:Button label="Button" />
 <mx:CheckBox label="Check box" />
 <mx:RadioButtonGroup id="cardType"/>
 <mx:RadioButton label="Visa" groupName="cardType" />
 <mx:RadioButton label="MasterCard" groupName="cardType"/>
 <mx:ComboBox dataProvider="{['a','b','c']}" />
 <mx:HSlider />
 <mx:TextInput />
</mx:VBox>
<mx:VBox horizontalAlign="left">
 <mx:List dataProvider="{['a','b','c']}" width="200"
   height="100" />
 <mx:ButtonBar dataProvider="{['a','b','c']}" />
 <mx:NumericStepper />
 <mx:Image source="@Embed('megan.jpg')" />
</mx:VBox>
</mx:Application>
```

When I run this in Flex Builder I see Figure 4-10.

As you would expect, in addition to these controls, you also have available labels with flat text and HTML, push buttons,

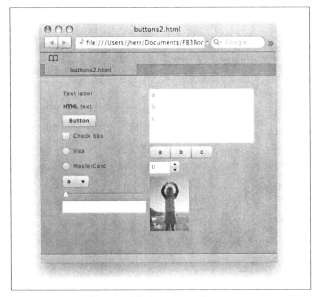

Figure 4-10. A collection of the basic control types

checkboxes and radio boxes, combos, text inputs, and lists, as well as some cool new controls such as sliders, numeric steppers, button bars, and images, among others.

Data Grids

We regularly have to build tables of structured information. This is easy in Flex, thanks to two controls: the DataGrid and the AdvancedDataGrid. I'll start by showing the DataGrid control (see Example 4-11).

Example 4-11. Datagrid.mxml

```
<?xml version="1.0" encoding="utf-8"?>
<mx:Application xmlns:mx="http://www.adobe.com/2006/mxml"
  layout="vertical">
 <mx:XMLList id="employees">
  <employee>
```

Figure 4-11. A simple data grid

```
  <name>Christina Coenraets</name>
  <phone>555-219-2270</phone>
  <email>ccoenraets@fictitious.com</email>
  <active>true</active>
 </employee>
 ...
</mx:XMLList>
<mx:DataGrid width="100%" height="100%" dataProvider=
  "{employees}">
 <mx:columns>
  <mx:DataGridColumn dataField="name" headerText="Name"/>
  <mx:DataGridColumn dataField="phone" headerText="Phone"/>
  <mx:DataGridColumn dataField="email" headerText="Email"/>
 </mx:columns>
</mx:DataGrid>
</mx:Application>
```

When I run this in Flex Builder I see Figure 4-11.

You don't even have to define the columns in the DataGrid unless you want to. The DataGrid control is smart enough to detect the columns from the data and set itself up if you haven't defined the columns.

The AdvancedDataGrid is just like the DataGrid but with a more powerful set of features. For example, it has the ability to roll up sections of the data and provide users with spinners so that they can drill down into the data.

Example 4-12 shows AdvancedDataGrid in action.

Example 4-12. Advgrid.mxml

```
<?xml version="1.0" encoding="utf-8"?>
<mx:Application xmlns:mx="http://www.adobe.com/2006/mxml"
  layout="vertical">
<mx:Script>
<![CDATA[
import mx.collections.ArrayCollection;
[Bindable]
private var dpHierarchy:ArrayCollection = new ArrayCollection([
  {Region:"Southwest", children: [ ... ]}
]);
]]>
</mx:Script>

<mx:AdvancedDataGrid width="100%" height="100%">
 <mx:dataProvider>
  <mx:HierarchicalData source="{dpHierarchy}"/>
 </mx:dataProvider>
 <mx:columns>
  <mx:AdvancedDataGridColumn dataField="Region"/>
  <mx:AdvancedDataGridColumn dataField="Territory_Rep"
   headerText="Territory Rep"/>
  <mx:AdvancedDataGridColumn dataField="Actual"/>
  <mx:AdvancedDataGridColumn dataField="Estimate"/>
 </mx:columns>
</mx:AdvancedDataGrid>
</mx:Application>
```

When I run this in the browser and click around a little bit I get something similar to Figure 4-12.

As with any control, you can use the itemRenderer functionality in Flex Builder to format each cell however you choose.

In-Place Editing

The DataGrid control also allows for editing cell contents in place. Example 4-13 shows just how easy this is.

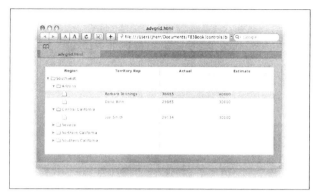

Figure 4-12. The advanced data grid

Example 4-13. Edit_table.mxml

```
<?xml version="1.0" encoding="utf-8"?>
<mx:Application xmlns:mx="http://www.adobe.com/2006/mxml"
  layout="vertical">
  <mx:XMLList id="customers" xmlns="">
    <customer><first>Jack</first>
    <last>Herrington</last></customer>
    <customer><first>Lori</first>
    <last>Herrington</last></customer>
    <customer><first>Megan</first>
    <last>Herrington</last></customer>
  </mx:XMLList>
  <mx:DataGrid dataProvider="{customers}" editable="true">
  <mx:columns>
    <mx:DataGridColumn dataField="first" />
    <mx:DataGridColumn dataField="last" />
  </mx:columns>
  </mx:DataGrid>
</mx:Application>
```

All I needed to do was add the **editable** attribute to the Data
Grid and set it to **true**.

When I bring this up in the browser and double-click on a cell,
I see something similar to Figure 4-13.

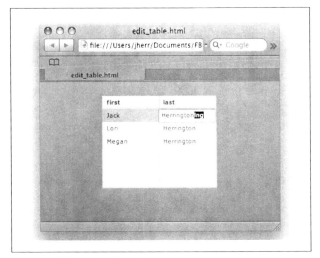

Figure 4-13. The editable grid

Of course, to make the example functional I would need to listen to the editing events and update the backend data store to match.

By default, the `DataGrid` uses a text editor to edit the cell contents, but you can provide your own editor renderer to use whatever controls you like to edit the value in the cell.

Tabs and Accordions

Sometimes you have more content than you can reasonably fit on the screen, so you need some way to let the user navigate around groupings of content. Flex provides several solutions, two of which, tabs and accordions, I'll demonstrate here.

Tabs are very easy to create, as you can see in Example 4-14.

Example 4-14. Tabs.mxml

```
<?xml version="1.0" encoding="utf-8"?>
<mx:Application xmlns:mx="http://www.adobe.com/2006/mxml"
  layout="vertical">
 <mx:TabNavigator borderStyle="solid" width="100%"
   height="100%">
   <mx:VBox label="Tab One">
     <mx:Label text="Tab one's content" />
   </mx:VBox>
   <mx:VBox label="Tab Two">
     <mx:Label text="Tab two's content" />
   </mx:VBox>
   <mx:VBox label="Tab Three">
     <mx:Label text="Tab three's content" />
   </mx:VBox>
 </mx:TabNavigator>
</mx:Application>
```

When I run this example from Flex Builder I see Figure 4-14.

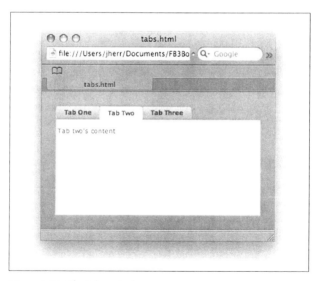

Figure 4-14. The tab control

Yep, it's really that easy. And you can reskin the tabs to be in whatever form you please with CSS and skinning (more on that shortly).

An accordion works exactly the same way, as you can see in Example 4-15.

Example 4-15. Accord.mxml

```
<?xml version="1.0" encoding="utf-8"?>
<mx:Application xmlns:mx="http://www.adobe.com/2006/mxml"
  layout="vertical">
 <mx:Accordion borderStyle="solid" width="100%" height="100%">
   <mx:VBox label="Tab One">
     <mx:Label text="Tab one's content" />
   </mx:VBox>
   <mx:VBox label="Tab Two">
     <mx:Label text="Tab two's content" />
   </mx:VBox>
   <mx:VBox label="Tab Three">
     <mx:Label text="Tab three's content" />
   </mx:VBox>
 </mx:Accordion>
</mx:Application>
```

All I did was change the tag name from TabNavigator to Accordion and the example works, as you can see in Figure 4-15. These are just two of the controls that you can use to manage the presentation of large sets of interface elements in a way that doesn't overwhelm the user.

Figure 4-15. The Accordion control

Menus

Flex also has support for menus, including those that appear at the top of the window as well as pop-up menus. Example 4-16 shows how to create a menu bar along the top of the window.

Example 4-16. Menu.mxml

```
<?xml version="1.0" encoding="utf-8"?>
<mx:Application xmlns:mx="http://www.adobe.com/2006/mxml"
  layout="absolute">
 <mx:MenuBar labelField="@label">
  <mx:XMLList>
   <menuitem label="File">
    <menuitem label="New" />
    <menuitem label="Open"/>
   </menuitem>
   <menuitem label="Edit"/>
   <menuitem label="Source"/>
```

```
  </mx:XMLList>
 </mx:MenuBar>
</mx:Application>
```

When I run this in Flex Builder I see something similar to
Figure 4-16.

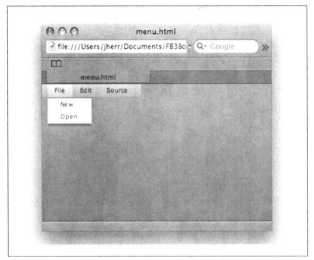

Figure 4-16. An example menu

There is also a handy control called `ApplicationControlBar`
that gives a nice-looking control set along the top of the window. Example 4-17 is the code for a sample `ApplicationControlBar`.

Example 4-17. Appbar.mxml

```
<?xml version="1.0" encoding="utf-8"?>
<mx:Application xmlns:mx="http://www.adobe.com/2006/mxml"
  layout="vertical">
<mx:ApplicationControlBar dock="true">
    <mx:ButtonBar dataProvider="{['People','Places',
      'Things']}" />
</mx:ApplicationControlBar>
</mx:Application>
```

When I launch this example in Flex Builder I see the nice presentation shown in Figure 4-17.

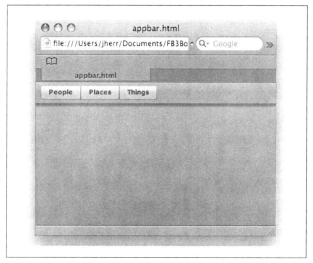

Figure 4-17. An application control bar

One thing I love about Flex is that even by default, it looks really good. I'm not a graphic designer by any stretch, so I like the fact that Figure 4-17 looks very slick but required absolutely no effort on my part.

Divider Boxes

Flex provides an easy way for your users to customize their own layout with divider boxes. The code in Example 4-18 shows just how easy it is to use a divider box.

Example 4-18. Divbox.mxml

```
<?xml version="1.0" encoding="utf-8"?>
<mx:Application xmlns:mx="http://www.adobe.com/2006/mxml"
  layout="horizontal">
```

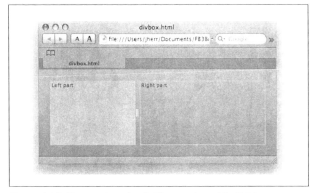

Figure 4-18. Two sections divided by an adjustable divider

```
<mx:HDividedBox width="100%" height="100%">
<mx:HBox backgroundColor="#ff9999" width="50%" height="100%"
  borderStyle="solid">
    <mx:Label text="Left part" />
</mx:HBox>
<mx:HBox width="50%" height="100%" borderStyle="solid">
    <mx:Label text="Right part" />
</mx:HBox>
</mx:HDividedBox>
</mx:Application>
```

When I run this in Flex Builder I see something similar to
Figure 4-18.

I can the drag the divider control to adjust the size of the left
and right parts to match my needs.

CSS

The best way to control the look of your Flex application is
through CSS. If you are familiar with CSS for HTML you will
find the CSS that's supported by Flex to be very familiar.

To demonstrate I'll take a very simple data entry form, make
the font size huge, and change the colors of the text inputs
based on CSS classes (see Example 4-19).

Example 4-19. CSS.mxml

```
<?xml version="1.0" encoding="utf-8"?>
<mx:Application xmlns:mx="http://www.adobe.com/2006/mxml"
  layout="absolute">
<mx:Style>
Application { font-size: 30; }
TextInput { color: #0000ff; }
.important { color: #ff0000; }
</mx:Style>
  <mx:Form>
    <mx:FormItem label="First Name">
      <mx:TextInput id="first" width="300" />
    </mx:FormItem>
    <mx:FormItem label="Last Name">
      <mx:TextInput id="last" width="300" />
    </mx:FormItem>
    <mx:FormItem label="Email">
      <mx:TextInput id="email" styleName="important"
        width="300" />
    </mx:FormItem>
    <mx:FormItem>
      <mx:Button label="Subscribe" />
    </mx:FormItem>
  </mx:Form>
</mx:Application>
```

The CSS styles are defined in the `mx:Styles` tag. I've defined three classes. The `Application` class, which controls all of the content within the `Application` tag, increases the font size. For the `TextInput` colors I specify that the text should be blue. For any control of the class `important`, the color should be red.

When I launch this in Flex Builder I see Figure 4-19 in my browser.

In this example, I've defined the CSS inline, but you can reference an external CSS file if you want to maintain styles across several applications. In addition, Flex Builder can help you manage your classes in Design mode.

Figure 4-19. A simple CSS example

Skinning

Flex also allows you to change the look of your whole application in a process called *skinning*. You can use CSS to apply new skins to your Flex controls. Skins are available for free as well as for purchase on the Web. A good repository for Flex skins is Scale Nine (*http://www.scalenine.com/*).

To demonstrate this I went to the Scale Nine website and found a pretty skin called "blue plastic." I downloaded the ZIP file and copied the contents into my Flex Builder 3 project folder via drag-and-drop.

I then modified my form by adding a `Panel` and replacing my own styles with a reference to the "blue plastic" skin (see Example 4-20).

Example 4-20. Styleform.mxml

```
<?xml version="1.0" encoding="utf-8"?>
<mx:Application xmlns:mx="http://www.adobe.com/2006/mxml"
  layout="vertical">
<mx:Style source="/blueplastic/blue_plastic.css" />
```

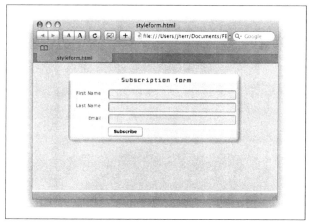

Figure 4-20. The skinned subscription form

```
<mx:Panel title="Subscription form" paddingTop="20">
  <mx:Form>
    <mx:FormItem label="First Name">
      <mx:TextInput id="first" width="300" />
    </mx:FormItem>
    <mx:FormItem label="Last Name">
      <mx:TextInput id="last" width="300" />
    </mx:FormItem>
    <mx:FormItem label="Email">
      <mx:TextInput id="email" styleName="important"
        width="300" />
    </mx:FormItem>
    <mx:FormItem>
      <mx:Button label="Subscribe" />
    </mx:FormItem>
  </mx:Form>
</mx:Panel>
</mx:Application>
```

Figure 4-20 shows the result.

As you can see, the panel has gotten a bit glossy. The font of the title of the panel has changed, and the background color for the entire design has also changed.

Filters and Effects

Flex supports a wide variety of filters and effects that you can apply to any user interface object. Take, for example, how easy it is to add a drop shadow to an image. The code for two images, one with a shadow and one without, appears in Example 4-21.

Example 4-21. Dropfilter.mxml

```
<?xml version="1.0" encoding="utf-8"?>
<mx:Application xmlns:mx="http://www.adobe.com/2006/mxml"
  layout="horizontal">
 <mx:Image source="@Embed('megan.jpg')" />
 <mx:Image source="@Embed('megan.jpg')">
   <mx:filters>
     <mx:DropShadowFilter />
   </mx:filters>
 </mx:Image>
</mx:Application>
```

It's almost as easy to apply filters and effects to text-based controls, but in many cases you'll have to embed the font. The result, when I look at it in the browser, looks like Figure 4-21.

Figure 4-21. The drop shadow filter applied to an image

You can also apply filters based on certain events, such as roll-overs, to provide interactive effects. Example 4-22 shows a button that glows when you roll your mouse pointer over it.

Example 4-22. Effect.mxml

```xml
<?xml version="1.0" encoding="utf-8"?>
<mx:Application xmlns:mx="http://www.adobe.com/2006/mxml"
  layout="horizontal">
 <mx:Button label="Push me!">
   <mx:rollOverEffect>
     <mx:Glow blurXTo="5" blurYTo="5" color="#ff0000" />
   </mx:rollOverEffect>
 </mx:Button>
</mx:Application>
```

As I roll my mouse pointer over the button, the effect looks similar to Figure 4-22.

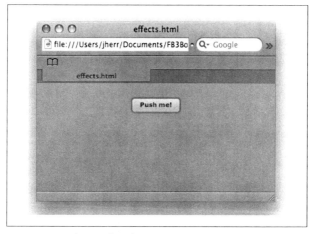

Figure 4-22. A button that glows

These kinds of effects can bring an interface to life for your customers. It's worth taking the time to learn how to use them effectively so that you have a complete set of tools at your disposal to make your applications grab people's attention.

CHAPTER 5

Working with the Server

Most Flex applications are going to work with a web server in some shape or form. Thankfully, Flex makes this very easy to do by providing a rich set of web service tools. In this chapter, I'll present two methods of accessing the server from a Flex application, and the server code that is required to support them.

You can access the server in a Flex application in five different ways:

POST or GET
> You can use a Flex application just as you would an HTML form. Flex can bundle up the elements in a form and post them to your web server application just as the browser would. Your application won't even know the difference.

Using HTTP services directly
> In a manner similar to Ajax, you can make an HTTP request of the server, even supplying POST content, and receive the response asynchronously. That response can be whatever flavor of data you want: text, XML, YAML, JSON, whatever you like. For JSON data the as3corelib library (*http://code.google.com/p/as3corelib/*) provides an excellent JSON interpreter.

SOAP
> Flex can access SOAP services directly using a set of Flex classes designed specifically for that purpose.

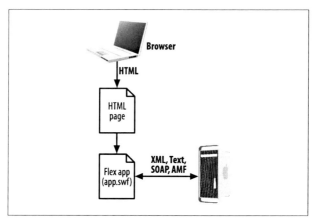

Figure 5-1. Flex-based network access

Remote objects

Flex applications can also make use of Flash's remoting capabilities by using remote objects. To make this happen the server code needs to support AMF requests. This is a proprietary binary format. Thankfully, there are libraries in each of the major languages to support AMF.

Directly through sockets

When all else fails you can use TCP/IP sockets directly and support whatever binary or ASCII protocol you choose.

I'll be showing only two examples in this chapter, but it's important that you know just how many ways Flash and Flex can communicate on the web.

Figure 5-1 shows how all of this fits together.

The HTML page loaded by the browser contains a reference to the Flash SWF file that contains the Flex application. That Flex application is loaded and run. It then makes requests directly to the server using a variety of transport protocols.

In the remainder of this chapter, I'll cover the POST/GET and HTTP service methods of accessing the server. I'll start with an example of using the POST/GET method.

POSTing to the Server with Flex

In this example, I'll post a simple subscription form to the server. The Flex code for the interface appears in Example 5-1.

Example 5-1. Form.mxml

```xml
<?xml version="1.0" encoding="utf-8"?>
<mx:Application xmlns:mx="http://www.adobe.com/2006/mxml"
  layout="absolute">
  <mx:HTTPService id="srv" url="http://localhost/formtest.php"
    method="POST"
    result="mx.controls.Alert.show
      (srv.lastResult.toString());">
    <mx:request>
      <first>{first.text}</first>
      <last>{last.text}</last>
      <email>{email.text}</email>
    </mx:request>
  </mx:HTTPService>
  <mx:Form>
    <mx:FormItem label="First Name">
      <mx:TextInput id="first"/>
    </mx:FormItem>
    <mx:FormItem label="Last Name">
      <mx:TextInput id="last"/>
    </mx:FormItem>
    <mx:FormItem label="Email">
      <mx:TextInput id="email"/>
    </mx:FormItem>
    <mx:FormItem>
      <mx:Button label="Subscribe" click="srv.send()"/>
    </mx:FormItem>
  </mx:Form>
</mx:Application>
```

This is pretty straightforward stuff. At the bottom of the application file is a big form tag that has all of the fields and the Subscribe button. At the top of the file is the definition for the HTTP service that will be called when the user clicks the Subscribe button.

The server code, shown in Example 5-2, is equally straightforward.

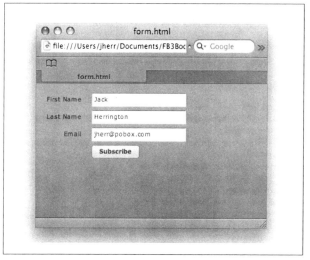

Figure 5-2. The form with my details in it

Example 5-2. Formtest.php

```php
<?php
echo( "Thanks ".$_REQUEST['first'] );
?>
```

When I run this example in Flex Builder it starts up with the empty form. I then fill in the form and see something similar to Figure 5-2.

When I click the Subscribe button the data is sent to the server. The HTTP service then fires the result event. That runs some code that I have defined in the HTTPService tag that will display the lastResult in an alert box. Figure 5-3 shows the result.

It doesn't get much easier than that!

Using the HTTPService Tag

The following is an embedded application created using Flex Builder. Users can type a five-digit zip code, such as 80401, and

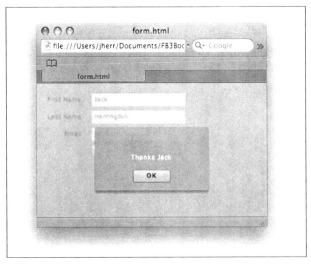

Figure 5-3. The alert that indicates a successful post

a shipping weight, such as 3, into the text boxes and click the Get Shipping Options button to retrieve and display the plain text data in a text box (see Figure 5-4).

Figure 5-4. The text return version of the application

A second version of the code will parse an XML response from the server and put it into a data grid. This ends up looking like Figure 5-5.

Stepping back from the user interface, let's look at how the Flex application communicates with the server. This interaction is shown in Figure 5-6.

Figure 5-5. The XML return version of the application

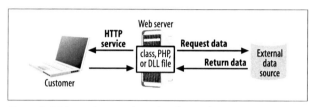

Figure 5-6. Network access from the Flex application

The Flex application, which is running on the customer's computer, uses the HTTPService tag to talk directly to the web server. The code on the web server, either in PHP, ASP, JSP, or something similar, talks to the database and then returns either text or XML.

Example 5-3 shows the code for the Flex application which responds to a text response from the web server.

Example 5-3. The text-based Flex application

```
<?xml version="1.0" encoding="utf-8"?>
<mx:Application xmlns:mx="http://www.adobe.com/2006/mxml"
 layout="absolute" backgroundColor="#FFFFFF"
   backgroundAlpha="0"
 backgroundImage="">
 <mx:Script>
```

```
  <![CDATA[
  import mx.rpc.events.ResultEvent;
  import mx.rpc.events.FaultEvent;
  import mx.controls.Alert;

  public function handlePlain(event:ResultEvent):void {
   shippingOptions.htmlText = event.result.toString();
  }

  public function handleFault(event:FaultEvent):void {
      Alert.show(event.fault.faultString, "Error");
  }
  ]]>
 </mx:Script>

 <mx:HTTPService result="handlePlain(event);"
    fault="handleFault(event);"
id="plainRPC" resultFormat="text"
  url="http://examples.adobe.com/flex3/exchangingdata/text
    /plainHttpService.php"
 useProxy="false">
  <mx:request xmlns="">
   <zipcode>{zipcode.text}</zipcode>
   <pounds>{weight_lb.text}</pounds>
  </mx:request>
 </mx:HTTPService>

 <mx:Label x="56" y="32" text="Zip Code" width="55"
    height="18"
textAlign="right" fontWeight="bold"/>
 <mx:Label x="56" y="58" text="Weight" width="55" height="18"
textAlign="right" fontWeight="bold"/>
 <mx:TextInput x="130" y="32" id="zipcode" width="160"
    height="22"/>
 <mx:TextInput x="130" y="58" id="weight_lb" width="160"
    height="22"/>
 <mx:Button x="130" y="95" label="Get Shipping Options"
click="plainRPC.send();" width="160" height="22"/>
 <mx:Text x="56" y="150" id="shippingOptions" width="310"
    height="133"
 fontWeight="bold"/>
</mx:Application>
```

The second version of the application, which handles parsing
the XML using ActionScript 3's E4X syntax, appears in Example 5-4.

Example 5-4. The XML version of the Flex application

```
<?xml version="1.0" encoding="utf-8"?>
<mx:Application xmlns:mx="http://www.adobe.com/2006/mxml"
  layout="absolute">

<mx:Script>
<![CDATA[
import mx.rpc.events.ResultEvent;
import mx.rpc.events.FaultEvent;
import mx.controls.Alert;

[Bindable]
private var shippingInfo:XMLList;

public function handleXML(event:ResultEvent):void {
  shippingInfo = event.result.option as XMLList;
}

public function handleFault(event:FaultEvent):void {
  Alert.show(event.fault.faultString, "Error");
}
]]>
</mx:Script>

 <mx:HTTPService result="handleXML(event);"
   fault="handleFault(event);"
 id="xmlRPC" resultFormat="e4x"
  method="POST" url="http://examples.adobe.com/flex3app
    /flex3samples/
exchangingdata/xml/xmlHttpService.jsp" useProxy="false">
  <mx:request xmlns="">
   <zipcode>{zipcode.text}</zipcode>
   <pounds>{weight_lb.text}</pounds>
  </mx:request>
 </mx:HTTPService>

 <mx:Label x="56" y="32" text="Zip Code" width="55"
   height="18" textAlign="right"
 fontWeight="bold"/>
 <mx:Label x="56" y="58" text="Weight" width="55" height="18"
   textAlign="right"
 fontWeight="bold"/>
 <mx:TextInput x="130" y="32" id="zipcode" width="160"
   height="22"/>
 <mx:TextInput x="130" y="58" id="weight_lb" width="160"
   height="22"/>
```

```
<mx:Button x="130" y="95" label="Get Shipping Options"
   click="xmlRPC.send();"
 width="160" height="22"/>
<mx:DataGrid dataProvider="{shippingInfo}"
   x="80" y="141" width="262" height="92"
     id="shippingOptionsList"
 editable="false" enabled="true">
  <mx:columns>
   <mx:DataGridColumn headerText="Service"
     dataField="service" />
   <mx:DataGridColumn headerText="Price" dataField="price" />
  </mx:columns>
 </mx:DataGrid>
</mx:Application>
```

Now that we have the Flex client side of the code, let's take a look at what we need on the server.

The Server Code in ColdFusion

You can write the server code in whatever server technology you like (e.g., PHP, Java, Rails, etc.). I've chosen to use Cold-Fusion here, but you can find the code for the other server models on the O'Reilly web page for this book.

The ColdFusion version of the text return page appears in Example 5-5.

Example 5-5. PlainHttpService.cfm

```
<cfsetting enablecfoutputonly="true" />
<cfinvoke component="Shipping"
  method="getShippingOptions" argumentcollection="#url#"
  returnvariable="myResult" />

<cfloop index="i" from="1" to="#ArrayLen(myResult)#">
    <cfoutput>#myResult[i].service#: #dollarFormat
      (myResult[i].price)#<br
 /></cfoutput>
</cfloop>
```

The XML version of the interface appears in Example 5-6.

Example 5-6. XmlHttpService.cfm

```
<cfsetting enablecfoutputonly="true" />

<cfsilent>
    <cfinvoke component="Shipping"
    method="getShippingOptions" argumentcollection="#url#"
    returnvariable="myResult" />
  <cfoutput>
    <cfxml variable="userXML">
      <options>
         <cfloop index="i" from="1" to="#ArrayLen(myResult)#">
              <option>
                  <service>#myResult[i].service#</service>
                  <price>#myResult[i].price#</price>
              </option>
         </cfloop>
      </options>
    </cfxml>
  </cfoutput>
</cfsilent>
<cfcontent reset ="yes" type="text/xml; charset=UTF-8">
<cfoutput>#userXML#</cfoutput>
```

The backend for the XML or plain text frontend appears in Example 5-7.

Example 5-7. Shipping.cfc

```
<cfcomponent>
    <cffunction name="getShippingOptions" access="remote"
    returntype="array">
        <cfargument name="zipcode" type="any" required="yes">
        <cfargument name="pounds" type="any" required="yes">
        <cfset var options=ArrayNew(1)>
        <cfset var baseCost=(zipcode / 10000) + (pounds * 5)>
        <cfset options[1] = structNew() />
        <cfset options[1].service="Next Day">
        <cfset options[1].price=baseCost * 4>
        <cfset options[2] = structNew() />
        <cfset options[2].service="Two Day Air">
        <cfset options[2].price=baseCost * 2>
        <cfset options[3] = structNew() />
        <cfset options[3].service="Saver Ground">
        <cfset options[3].price=baseCost>
        <cfreturn options>
    </cffunction>
```

```
<cffunction name="getShippingOptions_CFQuery" access=
  "remote" returntype="query">
    <cfargument name="zipcode" type="any" required="yes">
    <cfargument name="pounds" type="any" required="yes">
    <cfset var options=ArrayNew(1)>
    <cfset var baseCost=(zipcode / 10000) + (pounds * 5)>
     <cfscript>
   qOptions = queryNew("service, price");
   newRow = QueryAddRow(qOptions, 3);
        temp = QuerySetCell(qOptions, "service",
          "Next Day", 1);
        temp = QuerySetCell(qOptions, "price",
          baseCost * 4, 1);
        temp = QuerySetCell(qOptions, "service",
          "Two Day Air", 2);
        temp = QuerySetCell(qOptions, "price",
          baseCost * 2, 2);
        temp = QuerySetCell(qOptions, "service",
          "Saver Ground", 3);
        temp = QuerySetCell(qOptions, "price",
          baseCost, 3);
  </cfscript>
   <cfreturn qOptions>
  </cffunction>
</cfcomponent>
```

Going on from Here

As you can see, Flex makes it easy to communicate with your
web server no matter what protocol it's running. Protocols
such as SOAP and AMF are as easy to use as invoking a method
on an object. And the E4X syntax built into ActionScript 3
makes parsing XML directly a snap.

CHAPTER 6

More Flex Applications

This chapter will show some sample Flex applications to demonstrate various aspects of Flex development. You can use these examples as templates for your own applications.

A Runner's Calculator

Anyone who has taken up running as an exercise knows the pain of pushing to go too far too fast. It's commonly held wisdom that you should start at 1 mile and then go 10% farther every week. So, if you want to run 3.1 miles (5K) you should be training for 12 weeks.

To help calculate that number I've come up with a handy helper application written in Flex. The first draft of the code is shown in Example 6-1.

Example 6-1. Runner.mxml

```
<?xml version="1.0" encoding="utf-8"?>
<mx:Application xmlns:mx="http://www.adobe.com/2006/mxml"
  layout="absolute"
 creationComplete="onMilesChange(event)">
<mx:Script>
<![CDATA[
private function onMilesChange( event:Event ) : void {
 var miles:Number = parseFloat( txtMiles.text );
 var mile:Number = 1.0;
 var weeks:int = 0;
```

```
  while( mile < miles ) {
    weeks += 1;
    mile *= 1.1;
  }
  txtWeeks.text = weeks.toString();
}
]]>
</mx:Script>
 <mx:Form>
   <mx:FormItem label="Target Miles">
     <mx:TextInput id="txtMiles" change="onMilesChange(event)"
       text="3.1" />
   </mx:FormItem>
   <mx:FormItem label="Weeks">
     <mx:Label id="txtWeeks" />
   </mx:FormItem>
 </mx:Form>
</mx:Application>
```

The application is split into two pieces. The calculation function, onMilesChange, is located at the top of the script. The user interface is a form containing a text input for the number of miles and a label for the number of weeks. There is an event handler on the creationComplete event from the application which calls onMilesChange to do the initial calculation. There is also an event handler on the text field that calls onMilesChange whenever the change notification is fired.

Figure 6-1 shows the runner's calculator on startup.

I can change the target number of miles and watch as the number of weeks changes as a result. Figure 6-2 shows what happens when I change the target miles to 2.5.

It's nice to know the number of weeks, but what if I want to create a training calendar? I need to know the number of miles for each week as I go. I actually calculated the data I need in the onMilesChange function already; I just need to store it and display it somewhere. So, I'll update the Flex code a little bit, as shown in Example 6-2.

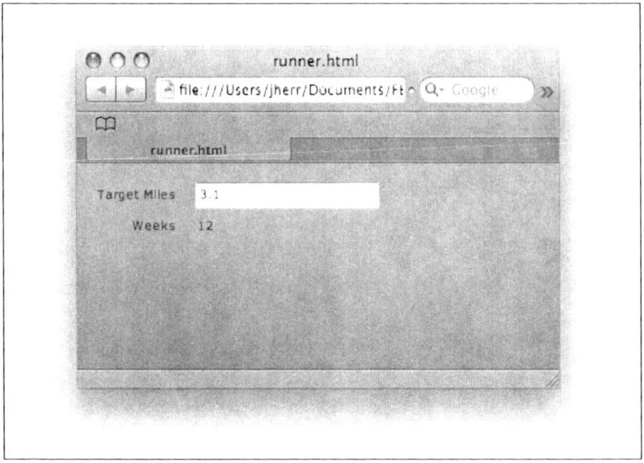

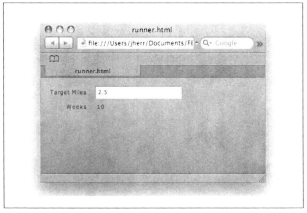

Figure 6-1. The runner's calculator after startup

Figure 6-2. The calculator after changing the target miles to 2.5

Example 6-2. Runner2.mxml

```
<?xml version="1.0" encoding="utf-8"?>
<mx:Application xmlns:mx="http://www.adobe.com/2006/mxml"
  layout="horizontal"
 creationComplete="onMilesChange(event)">
```

```
<mx:Script>
<![CDATA[
private function onMilesChange( event:Event ) : void {
 var miles:Number = parseFloat( txtMiles.text );
 var mile:Number = 1.0;
 var weeks:int = 0;
 var weekData:Array = [];
 while( mile < miles ) {
   weeks += 1;
   weekData.push( { week: weeks, miles: Math.round( mile * 10 )
     / 10 } );
   mile *= 1.1;
 }
 dgWeeks.dataProvider = weekData;
 txtWeeks.text = weeks.toString();
}
]]>
</mx:Script>
 <mx:Form>
   <mx:FormItem label="Target Miles">
     <mx:TextInput id="txtMiles" change="onMilesChange(event)"
       text="3.1" />
   </mx:FormItem>
   <mx:FormItem label="Weeks">
     <mx:Label id="txtWeeks" />
   </mx:FormItem>
 </mx:Form>
 <mx:DataGrid id="dgWeeks">
   <mx:columns>
     <mx:DataGridColumn dataField="week" headerText="Week" />
     <mx:DataGridColumn dataField="miles" headerText="Miles"/>
   </mx:columns>
 </mx:DataGrid>
</mx:Application>
```

In this new code, I've added an mx:DataGrid control which displays tabular data. In that grid I've defined two columns, one
for the week and another for the miles. Then in the onMile
sChange function I created an array called weekData which contains a list of objects that have week and miles values. I then set
the dataProvider of the data grid to the resultant array, and
voilà, I have a grid of the week and the number of miles.

Figure 6-3 shows the result.

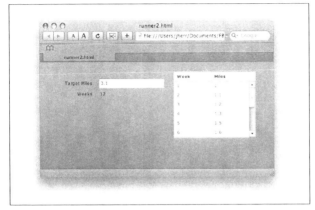

Figure 6-3. The calculator with the week table

Now I can build my training calendar using this handy tool. Of course, I can put an application such as this in any web page just like any other Flash movie. It's self-contained and ready to go.

A Simple Image Viewer

Web 2.0 is all about the media; images and video. So, it's a good thing that Flex makes it so easy to build Flash applications that use heaping helpings of both. I'll start by building a very simple image viewer that can look at a set of canned images (see Example 6-3).

Example 6-3. Pictures.mxml

```
<?xml version="1.0" encoding="utf-8"?>
<mx:Application xmlns:mx="http://www.adobe.com/2006/mxml"
  layout="horizontal"
 horizontalAlign="left">
<mx:Array id="images">
    <mx:String>megan1.jpg</mx:String>
    <mx:String>megan2.jpg</mx:String>
    <mx:String>megan3.jpg</mx:String>
    <mx:String>megan4.jpg</mx:String>
```

```
        <mx:String>megan5.jpg</mx:String>
    </mx:Array>
    <mx:List id="ctlImage" dataProvider="{images}"
        selectedIndex="0" width="100" />
    <mx:Image source="{ctlImage.selectedItem.valueOf()}"
        height="200" />
</mx:Application>
```

At the top of the application is the list of images—in this case, five images of my daughter Megan that I have included in the project by dragging and dropping them into Flex Builder in the *src* directory.

I then use an mx:List control to display the list of image names, and an mx:Image tag to display the currently selected image. Flex actually does the event handling to change the source of the image for me when the list changes.

When I run this from Flex Builder I see something similar to Figure 6-4.

Figure 6-4. The very simple image viewer

I can click on the list and see the different images that I have placed in the *src* directory with the MXML application. The images don't have to be local; they can be any URL, pointing to any server. So, the list could be a set of URLs to various images. And that list could easily be loaded from an external XML file using the HTTP support in Flex.

Back to the example at hand: I like the functionality, but the presentation is a little bland. So, let's make it more interesting by showing thumbnails of the images in the list. I do that in Example 6-4.

Example 6-4. Pictures2.mxml

```
<?xml version="1.0" encoding="utf-8"?>
<mx:Application xmlns:mx="http://www.adobe.com/2006/mxml"
  layout="horizontal"
 horizontalAlign="left">
<mx:Array id="images">
    <mx:String>megan1.jpg</mx:String>
    <mx:String>megan2.jpg</mx:String>
    <mx:String>megan3.jpg</mx:String>
    <mx:String>megan4.jpg</mx:String>
    <mx:String>megan5.jpg</mx:String>
</mx:Array>
<mx:List id="ctlImage" dataProvider="{images}"
  selectedIndex="0" width="50">
<mx:itemRenderer>
    <mx:Component>
        <mx:Image source="{data}" width="50" height="50" />
    </mx:Component>
</mx:itemRenderer>
</mx:List>
<mx:Image source="{ctlImage.selectedItem.valueOf()}"
  height="400" />
</mx:Application>
```

The only thing that has changed in this code is that I have added an itemRenderer to the list. That is an optional attribute that you can add to Flex controls so that you can render each cell in a table or list yourself. In this case, I provide an inline component that creates an mx:Image for each cell in the list.

I then run this in Flex Builder; the result appears in Figure 6-5.

Now I have thumbnails instead of images. Yes, it's really that easy. The item rendering and component support in Flex is

Figure 6-5. The image viewer with thumbnails

amazing, as you will learn as you delve more deeply into Flex. It's also something that is easy to support as you build your own controls.

Drag-and-Drop

Flex comes with a built-in drag-and-drop framework and many of the controls support drag-and-drop natively. Here is an example of dragging and dropping between two lists—one a list of things I like and the other a list of things I hate. The code for this appears in Example 6-5.

Example 6-5. Dragger.mxml

```xml
<?xml version="1.0" encoding="utf-8"?>
<mx:Application xmlns:mx="http://www.adobe.com/2006/mxml"
  layout="horizontal">
  <mx:Panel title="Things I like">
    <mx:List width="200" height="200"
        dragEnabled="true" dragMoveEnabled="true"
          dropEnabled="true">
      <mx:dataProvider>
        <mx:Array>
          <mx:String>Pizza</mx:String>
          <mx:String>Beer</mx:String>
          <mx:String>Football</mx:String>
          <mx:String>Thin Mints</mx:String>
        </mx:Array>
      </mx:dataProvider>
    </mx:List>
  </mx:Panel>
  <mx:Panel title="Things I hate">
    <mx:List width="200" height="200"
        dragEnabled="true" dragMoveEnabled="true"
          dropEnabled="true">
      <mx:dataProvider>
        <mx:Array>
          <mx:String>Working out</mx:String>
          <mx:String>Bad sci-fi</mx:String>
        </mx:Array>
      </mx:dataProvider>
    </mx:List>
  </mx:Panel>
</mx:Application>
```

To enable dragging I simply set the dragEnabled, dragMoveEna
bled, and dropEnabled attributes on the lists to true. Figure 6-6 shows the result.

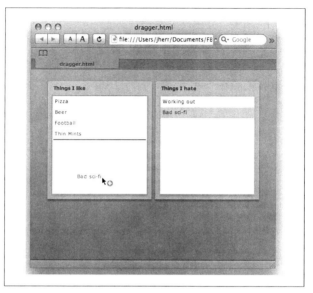

Figure 6-6. Dragging and dropping between two lists

This will add "Bad sci-fi" to the list of things I like.

I realize that this may seem like a silly example because you may have custom drag-and-drop requirements. But believe me when I tell you that building your own components so that they work with the drag-and-drop manager is very easy to do.

States and Transitions

Built into the core of the Flex API is support for different *states* in the user interface. For example, a box can be open or closed. Or a viewing area could be in two rows or three rows. You can define these states based on your needs and then set the parameters for each component that changes in each state.

To demonstrate I'll make a box that gets taller in the open state and shorter in the closed state. The example starts with a Flex application that references my open/close box that I call the **FlexiBox**. The code for the application appears in Example 6-6.

Example 6-6. States.mxml

```
<?xml version="1.0" encoding="utf-8"?>
<mx:Application xmlns:mx="http://www.adobe.com/2006/mxml"
  layout="horizontal"
  xmlns:mycomps="mycomps.*">
  <mycomps:FlexiBox />
</mx:Application>
```

FlexiBox is an MXML component that you create using the MXML Component command in the New menu item. The code for the **FlexiBox** appears in Example 6-7.

Example 6-7. FlexiBox.mxml

```
<?xml version="1.0" encoding="utf-8"?>
<mx:VBox xmlns:mx="http://www.adobe.com/2006/mxml" width="300"
  height="100"
  currentState="closed" cornerRadius="5" borderColor="#ff0000"
backgroundColor="#ffdddd"
  borderStyle="solid" borderThickness="3" paddingBottom="5"
    paddingLeft="5"
  paddingRight="5" paddingTop="5">
<mx:Script>
<![CDATA[
private function onChangerClick( event:Event ) : void {
  currentState = ( currentState == "open" ) ? "closed" :
    "open";
}
]]>
</mx:Script>
<mx:states>
  <mx:State name="open">
    <mx:SetProperty target="{this}" name="height"
      value="400" />
    <mx:SetProperty target="{btnChanger}" name="label"
      value="Close" />
  </mx:State>
  <mx:State name="closed">
    <mx:SetProperty target="{this}" name="height"
      value="100" />
    <mx:SetProperty target="{btnChanger}" name="label"
      value="Open" />
```

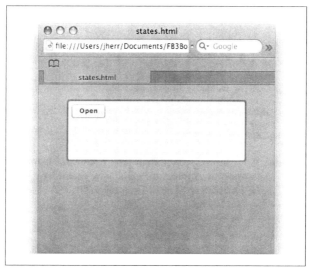

Figure 6-7. The closed state

```
    </mx:State>
  </mx:states>
  <mx:Button id="btnChanger" label="Open"
    click="onChangerClick(event);" />
</mx:VBox>
```

The important part of the code is the array of mx:State objects which define the two states: open and closed. In the open state the height of the control is set to 400, and in the closed state it's set to 100. The label of the Open/Close button is also changed from Open to Close based on the state.

When I bring this up in the browser the box starts in the closed state, as shown in Figure 6-7.

Then when I click the Open button the box gets big and the button changes to read Close because the button sets the cur rentState to open or closed depending on the current value (see Figure 6-8).

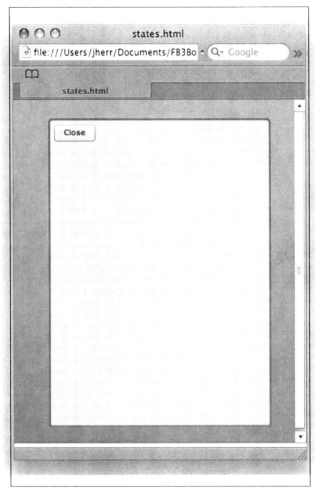

Figure 6-8. The open state

States make it easy to define how an interface can change in various modes. Transitions make the change between states *sexy* by applying effects to the change. To create these state transitions I've added a set of `mx:Transition` objects to the original example. That new application code appears in Example 6-8.

Example 6-8. States2.mxml

```
<?xml version="1.0" encoding="utf-8"?>
<mx:Application xmlns:mx="http://www.adobe.com/2006/mxml"
  layout="horizontal"
  xmlns:mycomps="mycomps.*">
  <mycomps:FlexiBox2 />
</mx:Application>
```

The new `FlexiBox` code appears in Example 6-9.

Example 6-9. FlexiBox2.mxml

```
<?xml version="1.0" encoding="utf-8"?>
<mx:VBox xmlns:mx="http://www.adobe.com/2006/mxml" width="300"
  height="100"
  currentState="closed" cornerRadius="5" borderColor="#ff0000"
 backgroundColor="#ffdddd"
  borderStyle="solid" borderThickness="3" paddingBottom="5"
    paddingLeft="5"
  paddingRight="5" paddingTop="5">
<mx:Script>
<![CDATA[
import mx.effects.easing.Bounce;
private function onChangerClick( event:Event ) : void {
  currentState = ( currentState == "open" ) ? "closed" :
    "open";
}
]]>
</mx:Script>
<mx:states>
  <mx:State name="open">
    <mx:SetProperty target="{this}" name="height"
      value="400" />
    <mx:SetProperty target="{btnChanger}" name="label"
      value="Close" />
  </mx:State>
  <mx:State name="closed">
    <mx:SetProperty target="{this}" name="height"
      value="100" />
    <mx:SetProperty target="{btnChanger}" name="label"
      value="Open" />
```

```
    </mx:State>
  </mx:states>
  <mx:transitions>
    <mx:Transition fromState="open" toState="closed">
      <mx:Parallel duration="500">
        <mx:SetPropertyAction target="{btnChanger}" />
        <mx:Resize target="{this}"
easingFunction="{mx.effects.easing.Bounce.easeOut}" />
      </mx:Parallel>
    </mx:Transition>
    <mx:Transition fromState="closed" toState="open">
      <mx:Parallel duration="500">
        <mx:SetPropertyAction target="{btnChanger}" />
        <mx:Resize target="{this}"
easingFunction="{mx.effects.easing.Bounce.easeOut}" />
      </mx:Parallel>
    </mx:Transition>
  </mx:transitions>
  <mx:Button id="btnChanger" label="Open"
    click="onChangerClick(event);" />
</mx:VBox>
```

Here I am specifying that the transition from open to closed
and vice versa should happen over the course of 500 milliseconds and should use a bouncing transition function. This
makes the box kind of jump up and down a little as it goes from
big to small and back to big again. It's fun to watch.

Transitions can make changes in the interface really fun to play
with. And building transitions in Flex is so easy you will find
yourself using them all the time.

A Simple Video Viewer

Sure, images are easy, but what about video? As it turns out,
video is pretty easy too. The first thing you have to do is to get
your videos into Flash Video (FLV) format. To do the conver-
sion I use an application called FFmpeg (*http://
ffmpeg.mplayerhq.hu/*). Well, actually I use a GUI wrapper for
the application called ffmpegx (*http://homepage.mac.com/ma
jor4/*) which runs on the Mac and handles all of the nasty com-
mand-line stuff for me. If video is a central focus of your

application, you'll want to look into Adobe's Flash Media Server which handles high volume video streaming.

Once I have my movies in FLV format, I put them up on my localhost site so that I can point a Flex `VideoDisplay` control at them. Unlike images, you can't point the video display at a local video resource without jumping through some security hoops.

The next step is to create the Flex application to display the video, as shown in Example 6-10.

Example 6-10. Movies.mxml

```
<?xml version="1.0" encoding="utf-8"?>
<mx:Application xmlns:mx="http://www.adobe.com/2006/mxml"
  layout="horizontal">
<mx:Array id="movieList">
    <mx:String>http://localhost/megan1.flv</mx:String>
    <mx:String>http://localhost/megan2.flv</mx:String>
    <mx:String>http://localhost/megan3.flv</mx:String>
</mx:Array>
<mx:VBox>
    <mx:List id="cntlMovie" dataProvider="{movieList}"
      width="300" />
    <mx:Button label="Pause" click="cntlDisp.pause();" />
    <mx:Button label="Play" click="cntlDisp.play();" />
</mx:VBox>
<mx:VideoDisplay id="cntlDisp"
  source="{cntlMovie.selectedItem.valueOf()}"
width="400" height="300" />
</mx:Application>
```

Just like with the image viewer, I have an array of movies at the top of the application. I then have a list control that shows the movies so that I can select them, as well as buttons to play and pause the video. Then, at the bottom of the file, I have the `VideoDisplay` control that does all of the hard work of showing the video.

When I launch this from Flex Builder I see the application shown in Figure 6-9.

I can select the movie I want to see, and then use the Play and Pause buttons to start and stop the playback. It is really this

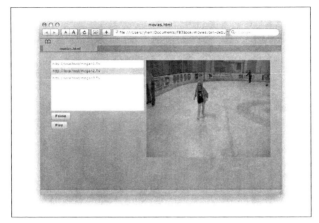

Figure 6-9. The simple multimovie player

easy to get started with video. From here you will likely want to add controls to move the playback point around, and respond to start and stop events generated by the control. But that requires only a little more code and a few more controls.

Creating Better Movies

The previous movie viewer had only Play and Pause buttons. Because video is such an important part of Flash work, I want to present a few more examples of how to use the `VideoDisplay` component.

This next example will show how to have a single Play/Pause button, how to build a scrubber to control the play head, and how to add a Rewind button. The code for this appears in Example 6-11.

Example 6-11. Bettermovie.mxml

```
<?xml version="1.0" encoding="utf-8"?>
<mx:Application xmlns:mx="http://www.adobe.com/2006/mxml"
  layout="vertical">
<mx:Script>
```

```
<![CDATA[
public function updateUI() : void {
    btnPlay.label = ( cntlDisp.playing ) ? 'Pause' : 'Play';
    sldCuePoint.value = cntlDisp.playheadTime;
}
public function onReady() : void {
    sldCuePoint.maximum = cntlDisp.totalTime;
    cntlDisp.play();
    updateUI();
}
public function onCueThumbPress( event:Event ) : void {
    cntlDisp.pause();
}
public function onCueThumbRelease( event:Event ) : void {
    cntlDisp.playheadTime = event.currentTarget.value;
}
public function onPlay() : void {
    if ( cntlDisp.playing ) cntlDisp.pause();
    else cntlDisp.play();
    updateUI();
}
]]>
</mx:Script>
<mx:VideoDisplay id="cntlDisp" source="http://localhost
  /megan2.flv" width="400"
 height="300"
    playheadUpdate="updateUI()" autoPlay="false"
      playheadUpdateInterval="150"
 ready="onReady()"
    live="false" rotation="-5">
<mx:filters>
    <mx:GlowFilter />
    <mx:DropShadowFilter />
</mx:filters>
</mx:VideoDisplay>
<mx:HBox>
    <mx:Button id="btnPlay" label="Pause" click="onPlay()" />
    <mx:Button label="Rewind" click="{cntlDisp.playheadTime =
      0;}" />
    <mx:HSlider id="sldCuePoint" liveDragging="true"
      allowTrackClick="false"
 thumbPress="onCueThumbPress(event);"
        thumbRelease="onCueThumbRelease(event);" />
</mx:HBox>
</mx:Application>
```

Figure 6-10. A movie player with reasonable controls

I also added a few effects (a rotation, glow, and drop shadow) to the video to demonstrate how you can create a more novel presentation for the movie using the power of Flash Player. This is shown in Figure 6-10.

If you wanted to you could even overlay the controls on the video and rotate the whole thing to give it a more interesting look. Another idea is to use the masking feature to show the video in a rough-edged container, or with a gradient alpha mask that would dim certain parts progressively.

The next example is an application that puts a text overlay on the video at certain cue points in the video. The code for this appears in Example 6-12.

Example 6-12. Cuemovie.mxml

```
<?xml version="1.0" encoding="utf-8"?>
<mx:Application xmlns:mx="http://www.adobe.com/2006/mxml"
```

```
  layout="vertical">
<mx:Script>
<![CDATA[
private var cues:Array = [
    { start: 0.0, stop: 1.0, text:'Megan' },
    { start: 4.0, stop: 7.0, text:'Swinging' }
];

public function updateUI() : void {
    btnPlay.label = ( cntlDisp.playing ) ? 'Pause' : 'Play';

    var found:Boolean = false;
    for each ( var cue:Object in cues ) {
        if ( cntlDisp.playheadTime.valueOf() >= cue.start &&
            cntlDisp.playheadTime.valueOf() <= cue.stop )
        {
            found = true;
            txtCueText.text = cue.text;
            cnvTextArea.visible = true;
        }
    }
    if ( !found )
        cnvTextArea.visible = false;
}
public function onReady() : void {
    cntlDisp.play();
    updateUI();
}
public function onPlay() : void {
    if ( cntlDisp.playing ) cntlDisp.pause();
    else cntlDisp.play();
    updateUI();
}
]]>
</mx:Script>
<mx:Canvas width="400" height="300">
<mx:VideoDisplay id="cntlDisp" source="http://localhost
  /megan2.flv" width="400"
 height="300" playheadUpdate="updateUI()" autoPlay="false"
playheadUpdateInterval="150"
 ready="onReady()"  live="false" />
<mx:Canvas id="cnvTextArea" width="400" height="30"
  backgroundAlpha="0.6"
 backgroundColor="black" top="270" visible="false">
    <mx:Text id="txtCueText" color="white" fontSize="18"
      fontWeight="bold" text="" />
</mx:Canvas>
```

Figure 6-11. A cue overlaid on top of the video display

```
</mx:Canvas>
<mx:HBox>
    <mx:Button id="btnPlay" label="Pause" click="onPlay()" />
    <mx:Button label="Rewind" click="{cntlDisp.playheadTime =
      0;}" />
</mx:HBox>
</mx:Application>
```

The `UpdateUI` method monitors the position of the play head and then shows or hides the overlay text depending on where the movie is in its playback. The overlay itself has a black background with an alpha so that you can still see the video through the overlay (see Figure 6-11).

Using the powerful states and transitions in Flex, you could easily have the cue pop out from below the video and then recede when the cue is no longer applicable.

CHAPTER 7

Advanced Flex Controls

As we already discussed, Flex has a lot of great controls baked right into it, including a chart control, an advanced grid control, accordions, layout managers, and a full set of basic controls. But even all of these might not satisfy your requirements. The good news is that there is a thriving community of open source and commercial groups building great components for Flex applications. This means you can build amazing applications without spending your time writing controls. This chapter provides a brief tour of some of these off-the-shelf controls.

ILOG Elixir

ILOG Visualization Products has developed a set of extremely powerful data visualization controls designed specifically for Flex. The ILOG Elixir toolkit (*http://www.ilog.com/products/ elixir/*) contains a complete set of 2D and 3D graph types, all of which allow you to create effects-based transitions that will make you look like a superstar. Included in the toolkit are ready-to-use schedule displays, map displays, dials, gauges, 3D and radar charts, Gantt charts, a treemap chart, and organization charts.

Figure 7-1 shows a 3D graph built using ILOG Elixir.

You can use the Flex controls on the right to adjust the ILOG graph to your taste. Source code is provided so that you can

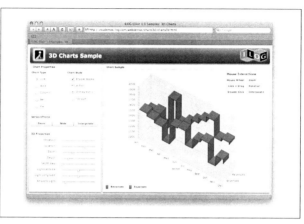

Figure 7-1. A 3D chart built with ILOG Elixir

copy and paste the graphing code directly into your application.

Figure 7-2 shows a combination of controls that includes a U.S. map displaying financial and sales data which in turn presents a set of pie charts representing sales objectives for each state. The gauge and radar charts are also shown here (the radar chart is the one in the middle of the bottom row).

As with Figure 7-1, the source code is provided so that you can use this in your own Flex application.

The last example I'll show (in Figure 7-3) is a treemap visualization of sales numbers that is commonly used to aggregate large data sets into a view that shows whether an area is active or inactive through the use of color.

Figure 7-2. An interactive map created with a combination of ILOG Elixir controls

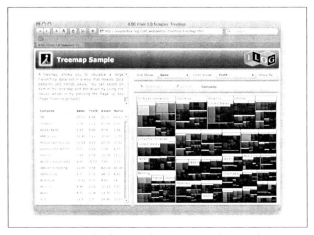

Figure 7-3. A sample of ILOG Elixir's treemap functionality

Figure 7-4. An example use of AFC components

ILOG Elixir is not free, but if highly customizable data visualization is a requirement for your Flex applications it's a lot easier to buy this package than it would be to write it yourself.

Advanced Flash Components

Flex is built on top of Flash, so you can use Flash components in your Flex application directly. This allows you to use a wide variety of off-the-shelf Flash components, including the Flash components available from Advanced Flash Components (AFC; *http://www.afcomponents.com/*). Figure 7-4 shows an application built using three of AFC's components: a scroll panel, a 2D carousel, and an enhanced tool tip control.

AFC also provides a mapping control that uses Google maps, as well as a 3D flow list similar to the Cover Flow 3D interface that you find in iTunes. And the company keeps developing new controls every few months.

In fact, the great thing about the Flex and Flash community is that components are being developed by open source and commercial groups all the time. Even if you don't find what you need today, you might find someone releasing it a month from now.

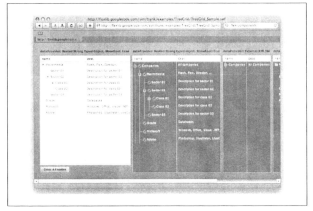

Figure 7-5. The enhanced tree control

The FlexLib Project

The FlexLib Project (*http://flexlib.googlecode.com/*) is an open source set of containers, controls, and classes to which you are free to contribute. The FlexLib Project comprises a wide variety of controls, including a horizontal accordion, advanced sliders and tab bars, and enhanced tree controls, among others. Figure 7-5 shows an example of an enhanced tree control showing some made up sample data.

FlexLib is a must-have for Flex developers. It's free; it comes with the source code, so you can see how these things are done; and it provides a wealth of great controls and classes that you can use right away.

Distortion Effects

Alex Uhlmann (*http://alex-uhlmann.de/flash/animationpack age/*) has developed a set of distortion effects to supplement the effects provided in the Flex core. Shown in Figure 7-6 is an example of the cube blur effect, which allows you to change

Figure 7-6. The cube distortion effect

between graphical elements, such as `TitleWindow`s, using a rolling cube effect.

He also provides movie-style effects, such as flipping and gating, and a wide variety of additional effects to jazz up your interface.

SpringGraph

Mark Shepherd has put together an amazing tree visualization tool called SpringGraph (*http://mark-shepherd.com/Spring Graph/*). Shown in Figure 7-7 is an example of his code pointed at Amazon's Apple iPod search.

This kind of visualization is ideal for social networks, graphing information relationships, and anything that is formed in a spider web of interrelated connections.

This chapter represented just a fraction of the Flex libraries and components that are available to you. You can find out more at *http://Flex.org/* and at FlexBox (*http://flexbox.mrinalwadh wa.com/*). Flex components are also available in the Flex components portion of the Adobe Exchange site at *http://www.Adobe.com/*.

Figure 7-7. The SpringGraph tree visualization tool

CHAPTER 8

Flex for Widgets

Flex 1 was primarily a server-based technology. Flex 2 allowed us to compile SWFs in Flex Builder and then deploy them. Flex 3 gives us a new feature called "runtime shared libraries" (RSLs), which means that the generated SWFs can be much smaller than in Flex 2—so small and self-contained that we can now use Flex Builder to create real widgets for websites. These RSLs contain the code for the Flex framework and are downloaded once to the client and then cached so that they don't have to be downloaded each time with the Flex application.

In this chapter, I'll walk you through creating a selection of widgets that you can use as templates for your own development.

Slide Show Widget

The first widget I'll build is a small slide show widget that reads an RSS feed from Flickr and displays the images one by one, switching out the image every two seconds. Example 8-1 shows the code for this application.

Example 8-1. Slideshow.mxml

```
<?xml version="1.0" encoding="utf-8"?>
<mx:Application xmlns:mx="http://www.adobe.com/2006/mxml"
  layout="absolute"
```

```
    paddingBottom="0" paddingLeft="0" paddingRight="0"
      paddingTop="0"
    creationComplete="flickReq.send();" backgroundAlpha="0"
      backgroundColor="white"
    backgroundGradientColors="[0xFFFFFF,0xFFFFFF]">
<mx:Script>
<![CDATA[
import mx.rpc.events.ResultEvent;
import mx.collections.ArrayCollection;
private var images:Array = [];
private var currentImage:int = 0;
private function onFetchResult( event:ResultEvent ) : void {
    var items:ArrayCollection = event.result.rss.channel.item as
      ArrayCollection;
    for each ( var item:Object in items )
        images.push( item.thumbnail.url.toString() );
    flickImg.source = images[currentImage];
    var t:Timer = new Timer( 2000 );
    t.addEventListener( TimerEvent.TIMER, onTimer );
    t.start();
}
private function onTimer( event:Event ) : void {
    currentImage += 1;
    if ( currentImage >= images.length )
        currentImage = 0;
    flickImg.source = images[currentImage];
}
]]>
</mx:Script>
<mx:HTTPService id="flickReq"
    url="http://api.flickr.com/services/feeds
      /photos_public.gne?format=rss_200_enc"
    result="onFetchResult(event)" />
<mx:Image width="100" height="100" id="flickImg">
<mx:filters><mx:DropShadowFilter /></mx:filters>
</mx:Image>
</mx:Application>
```

At the top of the application I define two methods. The first is
onFetchResult, which handles the response from Flickr and
sets up the list of images. The onFetchResult method also sets
up a timer that calls back to the onTimer method every 2,000
milliseconds (every two seconds) to change the source of the
image. The bottom portion of the example defines the HTTPSer

`vice` to connect to, and the image object to use to display the Flickr image.

Once I test this in the browser, I use the Project→Export Release Build command (shown in Figure 8-1) to build the release build of the slide show control.

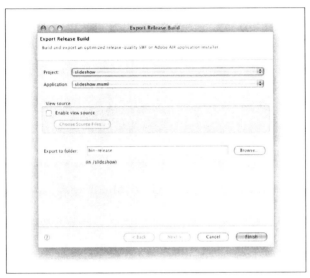

Figure 8-1. Exporting the release build

I then copy the exported *slideshow.swf* file into the same directory as the *index.html* file. The *index.html* file represents another web page that would reference the slide show. The *index.html* file is included in the source code download available on the O'Reilly website associated with this book.

Now I can test this out in my browser by just navigating to the file. Figure 8-2 shows the result.

This certainly is a nice little widget to fit on the page. But it's actually not a little widget when it comes to download size. It weighs in at 227 KB. Why? Because it's merging the Flex API

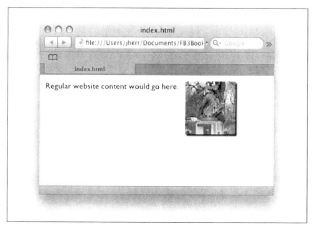

Figure 8-2. The slide show widget in action

code into the SWF. To reduce the size of the download we can have the *slideshow.swf* file reference an RSL library that holds the framework. Flash Player will download the RSL once and then cache it for future use.

To enable the RSL linking I go to the Properties dialog for the project and select Flex Build Path. I then click on the "Library path" tab and select the RSL option from the drop down. This is shown in Figure 8-3.

I navigate down to the *framework.swc* library just to make sure that it is indeed referencing the RSL. This is shown in Figure 8-4.

Figure 8-3. Selecting RSL linking

Figure 8-4. Ensuring the location of the RSL

Now when I export the release build, using the same mechanism as before, I get a *slideshow.swf* file that is 98 KB. That's far less than half the size of the original! To enable the client to use this I need to copy the *.swz* file for the framework into the same directory as the *.swf* file that references it.

Chat Widget

Reading stuff from the Web and displaying it is one thing. It's another thing to read and write data to a remote web server from a widget that is placed on any page. To show how to do this, I will create a very simple chat widget.

The first thing you have to understand is that for security reasons, a Flash movie on your machine cannot make an arbitrary request of just any URL. The Flash Player will first check for a *crossdomain.xml* file on the target host. The *crossdomain.xml* file (shown in Example 8-2) is telling Flash that "it's OK if you make a request of me."

Example 8-2. Crossdomain.xml

```
<?xml version="1.0"?>
<!-- http://www.adobe.com/crossdomain.xml -->
<cross-domain-policy>
<site-control permitted-cross-domain-policies="all"/>
  <allow-access-from domain="*" />
</cross-domain-policy>
```

On the server side, I'm going to use a combination of MySQL and PHP. The PHP code for the server is located in the code download associated with this book on the O'Reilly website.

The Flex code for the user interface appears in Example 8-3.

Example 8-3. Chat.mxml

```
<?xml version="1.0" encoding="utf-8"?>
<mx:Application xmlns:mx="http://www.adobe.com/2006/mxml"
  layout="vertical"
horizontalAlign="left" creationComplete="requestMessages();">
<mx:Script>
```

```
<![CDATA[
import mx.rpc.events.ResultEvent;
import mx.rpc.http.HTTPService;

private function sendMessage() : void {
    var message:String = txtMessage.text;
    message = message.replace( /[\r\n]/, '' );
    var sendReq:HTTPService = new HTTPService();
    sendReq.url = 'http://localhost/aschat
      /add.php?user='+escape(txtUser.text)+
'&message='+escape(message);
    sendReq.send();
}

private function messageKeyUp( event:KeyboardEvent ) : void {
    if ( event.keyCode == Keyboard.ENTER ) sendMessage();
}
private function requestMessages( event:Event = null ) : void {
    var msgReq:HTTPService = new HTTPService();
    msgReq.url = "http://localhost/aschat
      /messages.php?t="+((new Date()).valueOf());
    msgReq.resultFormat = 'e4x';
    msgReq.addEventListener(ResultEvent.RESULT,
      onMessageFetchResult);
    msgReq.send();
}
private function onMessageFetchResult( event:ResultEvent ) :
  void {
    var messages:Array = [];
    for each ( var msg:XML in event.result..message ) {
        var message:String = msg.text();
        message = message.replace( /[\r\n]/, '' );
        messages.push( { user: msg.@user, message: message } );
    }
    msgGrid.dataProvider = messages;
    var t:Timer = new Timer( 1000, 1 );
    t.addEventListener(TimerEvent.TIMER, requestMessages );
    t.start();
}
]]>
</mx:Script>
<mx:DataGrid id="msgGrid" width="260" height="400">
<mx:columns>
    <mx:DataGridColumn dataField="user" headerText="User"
      width="60" />
    <mx:DataGridColumn dataField="message"
      headerText="Message" width="200" />
```

```
    </mx:columns>
  </mx:DataGrid>
  <mx:Form width="260">
    <mx:FormItem label="User">
        <mx:TextInput id="txtUser" text="Jack" />
    </mx:FormItem>
    <mx:FormItem label="Message">
        <mx:TextInput id="txtMessage" text=""
          keyUp="messageKeyUp(event);" />
    </mx:FormItem>
  </mx:Form>
</mx:Application>
```

This looks like a complicated application, but it really isn't. On the bottom of the file is the user interface, which starts with the data grid that shows the messages and then finishes with a form that has text fields for the username and the message to send.

The methods for the chat system start at the top of the file. The sendMessage method creates a request to run the *add.php* script on the server with the current contents of the User and Message fields. This sendMessage script is run when the user presses the Enter key after entering text in the text field. The message KeyUp method looks for the user pressing Enter.

The requestMessages and onMessageFetchResult methods deal with getting data from the server. The requestMessages method starts the request. The onMessageFetchResult message parses the response and starts a timer that will initiate another request when the timer goes off.

When I start the chat widget in my browser I see something similar to Figure 8-5.

I then type a message into the Message field and press Enter. That starts the request to *add.php*. After the timer goes off, the chat widget requests the current messages from the server and puts the current list in the grid.

As with the other widgets, you can put this control onto any page if you've properly installed the *crossdomain.xml* file in the target PHP server.

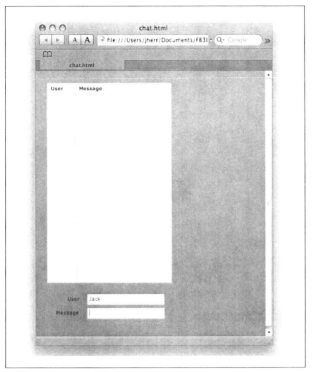

Figure 8-5. The startup chat widget

CHAPTER 9

Flex on AIR

Adobe's AIR runtime is your ticket to the world of cross-platform desktop application development. And the great news is that you can use the tools you already know. AIR supports building desktop applications in either Flex or DHTML. In this chapter, I'll concentrate on the use of Flex.

Creating an AIR Version of the Runner's Calculator

The process starts with creating an AIR project in Flex Builder. Use the New→Project menu item as you normally would. Then select "Desktop application" instead of "Web application", as I have done in Figure 9-1.

I'm going to create an AIR version of the runner's calculator example from Chapter 3. Once I've created the AIR project using the New MXML Project command, I copy all of the content from my original runner application, except for the `mx:Application` tag, into the *AIR_runner.mxml* file. This is shown in Example 9-1.

Example 9-1. AIR_runner.mxml

```
<?xml version="1.0" encoding="utf-8"?>
<mx:WindowedApplication xmlns:mx="http://www.adobe.com
  /2006/mxml"
```

Figure 9-1. The Project dialog with AIR selected

```
layout="horizontal"
 creationComplete="onMilesChange(event)">
<mx:Script>
<![CDATA[
private function onMilesChange( event:Event ) : void {
 var miles:Number = parseFloat( txtMiles.text );
 var mile:Number = 1.0;
 var weeks:int = 0;
 var weekData:Array = [];
 while( mile < miles ) {
   weeks += 1;
   weekData.push( { week: weeks, miles: Math.round
     ( mile * 10 ) / 10 } );
   mile *= 1.1;
 }
 dgWeeks.dataProvider = weekData;
 txtWeeks.text = weeks.toString();
}
]]>
</mx:Script>
 <mx:Form>
   <mx:FormItem label="Target Miles">
     <mx:TextInput id="txtMiles" change="onMilesChange(event)"
```

```
      text="3.1" />
  </mx:FormItem>
  <mx:FormItem label="Weeks">
    <mx:Label id="txtWeeks" />
  </mx:FormItem>
</mx:Form>
<mx:DataGrid id="dgWeeks">
  <mx:columns>
    <mx:DataGridColumn dataField="week" headerText="Week" />
    <mx:DataGridColumn dataField="miles" headerText="Miles"/>
  </mx:columns>
</mx:DataGrid>
</mx:WindowedApplication>
```

I could have created a component and shared that between the web version and the AIR version. But I wanted to focus this example on building AIR applications and not on the benefits of reusable MXML components.

The next thing I need to do is to make some small changes to the *AIR_Runner-app.xml* that was generated when the *AIR_Runner-app.mxml* file was created. The AIR loader application uses this XML file when it starts up. It's populated with all the biographical information about the application: the path to the SWF, the dimensions of the startup window, the icon if you have one, the name of the application, and so on.

I tweak only three things: the name of the window, and its height and width, as shown in Example 9-2.

Example 9-2. Selected segments of AIR_Runner-app.xml

```
...
        <title>Runner's Calculator</title>
        <width>600</width>
        <height>250</height>
...
```

Then I run the AIR application in Flex Builder just as I would any web application that I develop using Flex. You can see the result of this in Figure 9-2.

Your customers who want to run this application are first going to have to install the AIR runtime on their computer. They can

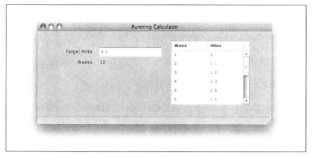

Figure 9-2. The desktop runner's calculator

get that from Adobe (*http://adobe.com/air*), and you can link to it on your website. Once they have AIR installed, you can use Flex Builder to package up an AIR application into a single file and send it to them or post it on the Web.

There is a lot more to AIR than what I covered in this short walkthrough. AIR has extra APIs that you can use to get access to the local filesystem, create subwindows, access local devices, and more. In addition, you can bind in your own platform-specific APIs to get access to any specialized API you want. Adobe's AIR site is your starting point for all the information you need on this powerful API.

CHAPTER 10

Resources for Flex Developers

In addition to the resources I already talked about, lots of additional resources are available from which you can learn more about Flex. I'll cover a few of them in this chapter; these will surely lead you to even more sources of information.

Getting connected as a Flex developer starts with subscribing to the mailing lists provided by Adobe. These are low-traffic, high-quality, spam-free lists where Adobe posts all kinds of up-to-date information.

Flex Websites

There are two websites you really need to know about. Flex.org (*http://flex.org*) is a community site for Flex developers, and has links to all sorts of great resources for Flex developers. The Flex Developer Center (*http://developer.adobe.com/flex*) is the official Adobe Flex community center and has tons of articles and great information for Flex developers.

Blogs and Sites

I consider the Flex blogs to be a primary source of information on Flex. Often, blog entries include code recipes that are too small to warrant coverage in an article, but are nonetheless helpful and will save you the time and effort of researching and implementing Flex solutions yourself. Here's a list of what I consider to be some of the best Flex blogs out there:

Flex Team Blog (http://weblogs.macromedia.com/flexteam/)
> This is the official blog from the Flex team at Adobe.

Mike Morearty (http://www.morearty.com/blog/)
> Mike is the brains behind the debugging portion of Flex Builder. His blog keeps you up-to-date on what's happening in the world of Flex.

Chet Haase (http://graphics-geek.blogspot.com/)
> Chet's blog specializes in Flex/Flash graphics techniques.

Narciso Jaramillo (http://www.rictus.com/muchado/)
> NJ is a Flex expert and a great writer who is very funny.

Jack Herrington (http://jackherrington.com/)
> I've heard this guy has a pretty good Flex blog (and that he writes a good Flex book as well).

If you like podcasts, you can subscribe to a weekly Flex podcast on iTunes (*http://www.apple.com/search/ipoditunes/?q=flex +broadcast*). You can also subscribe to "The Flex Show" (*http://www.theflexshow.com/*).

You can also learn a lot more about Flex and rich Internet application (RIA) development in general at these sites:

RIAForge (http://www.riaforge.org/)
> Hosts several open source development projects for Flex

Flex.org (http://flex.org)
> The Flex community website

InsideRIA (http://www.insideria.com/)
> O'Reilly's RIA website

The Flex Cookbook

The Flex Cookbook is an invaluable resource for both Flex beginners and experienced Flex coders. It's a community-driven repository of code fragments for Flex that solves lots of common coding problems. If you are stumped on how to do something, the first place you will want to visit is the Flex Cookbook (*http://www.adobe.com/go/flex_cookbook*).

When you think you are ready and have something to contribute, you can add recipes to the Cookbook as well to give something back to the community.

The Flex Cookbook home page even offers an Eclipse plug-in that will show you the most recent Cookbook entries in Flex Builder.

Community Resources

Several Flex community resources are also available. One is the Flex Support Forums (available at *http://www.adobe.com/go/flex_forums*), where you can find user-to-user discussions regarding Flex. What's more, the Flex team monitors the forums to help you out when you get into a jam.

Also, it's a good idea to join a local Flex user group. Flex user groups are located all over the world and are cataloged at *http://flex.org/community/*. Meanwhile, a Flex "Camp"—which is an informal gathering of Flex enthusiasts and Adobe folks who get together to try to build real Flex applications—should be high on your list of things to attend. You can find out when a Flex Camp is coming to your town by visiting the Flex.org Camp page (*http://flex.org/camp/*). There are also conferences, such as the 360|Flex conference (*http://www.360conferences.com/360flex/*), to attend if you are in the area.

If you want to find a job in which you can put your knowledge of Flex to good use, the Flex.org (*http://flex.org*) site also has information on the current Flex job market.

Books

Besides this book, lots of books on Flex 3 and ActionScript 3 are currently available. One that I strongly recommend is *Flex 3 Cookbook*. Its sister publication, *ActionScript 3 Cookbook*, is also an excellent resource, as is *Essential ActionScript 3*, which demonstrates use of ActionScript that will blow your mind (all three books are published by O'Reilly). *Essential ActionScript 3* also provides excellent coverage on using E4X, which is critical if you are doing a lot of XML work. And be sure to check out *Programming Flex 3* (O'Reilly), scheduled for publication later this year, for lots of up-to-date information on using the Flex 3 framework to build Flash-based web and desktop applications. You can check Flex.org (*http://flex.org*) for a complete list of books for Flex developers.

Index

Symbols

2D graph type, 99
3D graph type, 99

A

absolute positioning (Canvas container), 39
absolute property (Application container), 36
accordions, 53–56
Advanced Flash Components (AFC), 102
AdvancedDataGrid control, 49–53
AFC (Advanced Flash Components), 102
AIR, 7, 117–120
  desktop applications and, 16
AMF requests, 66
application container, 35

Application tag, 21
  CSS and, 60
applications, 7–18
  constructing, 19–34
  online, 9–11
ArrayCollection statement, 24
as3corelib library, 65
aviary, 10

B

backgroundGradientColors attribute (Application), 21
backgroundGradientColors parameter, 36
bindable private variables, 25
bottom property (Canvas container), 41
Box class, 37–39
buttons, 48
Buzzword project, 11

We'd like to hear your suggestions for improving our indexes. Send email to *index@oreilly.com*.

VideoDisplay component, 93
VideoDisplay control, 92

W
widgets, 12, 107–114

Y
YourMinis portal, 13

The Adobe Developer Library Guide for
Rich Internet Application Developers

Flex™ 3
Cookbook™

Joshua Noble &
Todd Anderson

O'REILLY®

Adobe
Developer
Library

This highly practical book contains more than 200 proven recipes for developing interactive Rich Internet Applications and Web 2.0 sites. You'll find everything from Flex basics and working with menus and controls, to methods for compiling, deploying, and configuring Flex applications. Each recipe features a discussion of how and why it works, and many of them offer sample code that you can put to use immediately.

Joshua Noble is a development consultant with three years of experience in building enterprise level applications using Flex integrated with Java, Ruby, ColdFusion, and Microsoft .NET.

Todd Anderson is a Senior Software Developer in the Multimedia Platforms Group at Schematic Boston, and is co-author of *Adobe AIR Instant Results* (Wrox/Wiley).

Programming Flex 3 *is the definitive guide to creating rich media applications with Adobe's new open source Flex 3 platform.*

This is the complete update for Flex 3 of the bestselling *Programming Flex 2*, the definitive introduction to Flex for developers. This book fills in the gaps of the official Flex documentation and helps developers get comfortable quickly with Flex 3.

Joey Lott is the author or co-author of *Flash 8 Cookbook, Programming Flash Communication Server,* and *ActionScript 3.0 Cookbook* (all O'Reilly). He has been teaching Flash and ActionScript since 1999.

Chafic Kazoun is the founder and Chief Software Architect at Atellis, and is widely considered one of the world's top experts on Flex. He has worked with Flex since its inception, and maintains a busy speaking and consulting schedule.

www.oreilly.com

Programming

Flex™ 3

O'REILLY®

Adobe
Developer
Library

*Chafic Kazoun
& Joey Lott*

A beginner's guide to Adobe Flex 3, this book offers hands-on instruction for developing Rich Internet Applications.

With this book's unique, hands-on approach, you will be able to tinker with examples right away, and create your own Rich Internet Applications with Flex within the first few chapters. *Learning Flex 3* offers step-by-step instructions that are clear and concise; that teaches you how to build a layout, add interactivity, work with data, and deploy your applications to either the Web or the desktop.

Alaric Cole has been working with Flash technologies since the introduction of ActionScript. Once Flex came on the scene, he's been focused primarily on Flex development, creating enterprise applications with rich data visualization, interactive media, and advanced user interface components. Pushing Flex beyond its comfort zone, he has worked with Adobe to discover ways to improve the technology.

Learning Flex 3

GETTING UP TO SPEED WITH RICH INTERNET APPLICATIONS

Alaric Cole

Adobe Developer Library

O'REILLY

Written by members of Adobe's AIR product team, this is the official guide to version 1.0 of the new Adobe Integrated Runtime (AIR).

This book explains how you can use AIR to build and deploy HTML and JavaScript-based web applications to the desktop, using the tools and technologies with which you may already be familiar.

Mike Chambers, senior product manager for developer relations for AIR, has spent the last 8 years building applications that target the Flash runtime.

Daniel Dura is a Platform Evangelist at Adobe focusing on AIR and Flash.

Kevin Hoyt is also a Platform Evangelist at Adobe.

Dragos Georgita is an engineer on the Adobe AIR team, leading a group that focuses on Ajax support in the runtime.

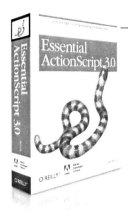

Written by the one and only Colin Moock, this is the top-selling ActionScript book of all time, and considered the authoritative resource.

More than two years in the making, ActionScript 3.0 presents perhaps the most substantial upgrade to Flash's programming language ever. The enhancements to ActionScript's performance, feature set, ease of use, cleanliness, and sophistication are simply staggering. Revolutionary improvements abound. *Essential ActionScript 3.0* focuses on the core language and object-oriented programming with coverage of the Flash Player API.

Colin Moock is an independent ActionScript expert whose world-renowned books have educated Flash programmers since 1999.

> "Few Flash books are as anticipated as the ones from Colin Moock, and this one has been in the works for more than two years. It's worth the wait and Colin once again proves that his book should be on every developer's desk."
>
> flashmagazine.com

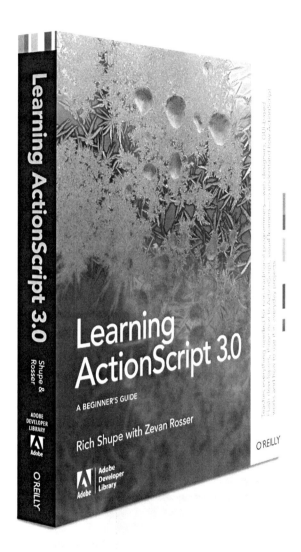

"The best ActionScript book ever written."

Lee Brimelow, Platform Evangelist at Adobe

Teaches web designers, GUI-based Flash developers, and those new to ActionScript everything they need to know to understand how ActionScript works, and how to use it in their everyday projects.

Learning ActionScript 3.0 gives you a solid foundation in the Flash language and demonstrates how you can use it for practical, everyday projects. The book gives you a clear look into essential topics such as logic, event handling, displaying content, migrating legacy projects to ActionScript 3.0, classes, and much more. Written for those new to the language, it helps you expand your skill-set by first focusing on clear, concise examples in the timeline, evolving into OOP examples over time—allowing you to choose the programming approach with which you are most comfortable.

Rich Shupe has been designing and developing with Flash since it was called FutureSplash, and is a recognized authority on several technologies, including Flash, Director, and QuickTime. In addition to his production experience, Rich has been teaching professionally for 10 years, and is a full-time faculty member at New York's School of Visual Arts' Computer Art Dept.

Zevan Rosser is a freelance designer/programmer/consultant and computer artist. He teaches ActionScript and Flash animation at New York's School of Visual Arts and FMA. When he's not working on commercial projects he works on his personal site, www.shapevent.com.

This hands-on introduction to design patterns is for experienced Flash and Flex developers ready to tackle sophisticated programming techniques with ActionScript 3.0.

If you're an experienced Flash or Flex developer ready to tackle sophisticated programming techniques with ActionScript 3.0, this hands-on introduction to design patterns takes you step by step through the process. You learn about various types of design patterns and construct small abstract examples before trying your hand at building full-fledged working applications outlined in the book.

Dr. William B. Sanders is a Professor of Interactive Information Technology at the University of Hartford. He has published 44 computer and computer-related books, written software ranging from Basic to Flash Media Server ActionScript and served as a consultant for several computer software companies.

Dr. Chandima Cumaranatunge is an Assistant Professor of Interactive Information Technology at the University of Hartford. He teaches an introduction to the IIT major, covering Flash and some ActionScript, a gaming course using Flash and ActionScript and educational technology courses in the Education, Nursing, and Health Professions College. Recently he received a grant to teach an experimental course in robotics.

"This book is a useful guide for approaching programming problems and challenges in Flash and Flex applications through the use of reusable design patterns in
ActionScript 3.0. The authors show, step by step, how
to structure programming code that can be used to
build working applications. The reader is introduced
to progressively more complex programming examples that provide insight into producing well-struc-
tured programming solutions."

Michael Kleper, The Kleper Report on Digital Publishing